TODD HAMPSON and JEFF KINLEY

THE PROPHECY PROS'
ILLUSTRATED
GUIDE to Tough Questions About the

END
TIMES

HARVEST PROPHECY
AN IMPRINT OF HARVEST HOUSE PUBLISHERS

Cover by Kyler Dougherty; interior design by Chad Dougherty

Cover art © by Todd Hampson

Published in association with William K. Jensen Literary Agency, 119 Bampton Court, Eugene, Oregon 97404.

For bulk, special sales, or ministry purchases, please call 1-800-547-8979. Email: Customerservice@hhpbooks.com

Prophecy Pros' Illustrated Guide to Tough Questions About the End Times

Copyright © 2021 Text © by Jeff Kinley and Todd Hampson. Artwork © by Todd Hampson.
Published by Harvest House Publishers
Eugene, Oregon 97408
www.harvesthousepublishers.com

ISBN 978-0-7369-8367-9 (pbk)
ISBN 978-0-7369-8368-6 (eBook)

Library of Congress Cataloging-in-Publication Data

Names: Kinley, Jeff, author. | Hampson, Todd, author.
Title: Prophecy pros illustrated guide to tough questions about the end
    times / Jeff Kinley and Todd Hampson. "Description: Eugene, Oregon : Harvest House Publishers, [2021] |
Includes
    bibliographical references. | Summary: "Packed with helpful charts,
    infographics, timelines, and illustrations, the Prophecy Pros
    Illustrated Guide to Tough Questions About the End Times delivers
    to-the-point, speculation-free, biblically sourced answers about the
    rapture, second coming, God's plans for Israel, the tribulation, life in
    heaven, and beyond"—Provided by publisher.
Identifiers: LCCN 2020047156 (print) | LCCN 2020047157 (ebook) | ISBN
    9780736983679 (trade paperback) | ISBN 9780736983686 (ebook)
Subjects: LCSH: Bible—Prophecies. | Prophecy pros (Podcast) | End of the
    world—Biblical teaching. | Eschatology—Biblical teaching. |
    Prophecy—Christianity—Biblical teaching.
Classification: LCC BT877 .K5625 2021 (print) | LCC BT877 (ebook) | DDC
    236/.9—dc23
LC record available at https://lccn.loc.gov/2020047156
LC ebook record available at https://lccn.loc.gov/2020047157

Printed in the United States of America

24 25 26 27 28 29 / VP-CD / 10 9 8 7 6 5 4

Dedicated to all those in the body of Christ
who hunger for God's truth
and eagerly await Jesus' return.

In the future there is reserved for me the crown of righteousness,
which the Lord, the righteous Judge,
will award to me on that day; and not only to me,
but also to all who have loved His appearing.

—2 Timothy 4:8

ACKNOWLEDGMENTS

We would like to acknowledge Bob Hawkins, Sherrie Slopianka, Don Sage, Steve and Becky Miller, Kari Duffy, and the rest of the visionaries at Harvest House Publishers.

CONTENTS

CHAPTER 1

THE BASICS OF BIBLE PROPHECY

#1 What Is Bible Prophecy?

In the world of Bible prophecy, there is no shortage of sensationalism. From doomsday preachers to quirky "prophecy nerds" propagating conspiracy theories about Antichrist and clandestine secret societies to bestselling books on the subject, prophecy is in the air.

Even so, at times it seems there's more confusion than clarity. With a multitude of voices teaching a wide array of beliefs, theories, and interpretations, it can rapidly turn biblical truth into static noise. But this is not the way God intended it.

Though certain prophecies do require deeper study than others, on the whole, prophecy itself can be relatively easy to grasp...*if* you know what you're doing.

Bible prophecy is simply God's plan revealed ahead of time. Like a movie trailer, it's a sneak preview of things to come. But unlike a fictional movie, prophecy tells us what's *actually* going to happen. That's why some have referred to it as history written in advance.

In the Old Testament, prophets were given truth about the nation Israel and the future Messiah—His birth, ministry, death, and resurrection. In the New Testament, John the Baptist, Jesus, Paul, Peter, and John made prophecies that addressed, from their perspectives, events that would take place in both the near and far future.

In the last book in the Bible, we encounter an entire catalog of prophecies that have yet to be fulfilled. In fact, Revelation is 95 percent prophecy (Revelation 1:19). And only God can accurately foretell the future—not psychics, soothsayers, or even Satan himself.

The prophet Daniel echoed this truth: "There is a God in heaven who reveals mysteries, and He has made known to King Nebuchadnezzar what will take place in the latter days" (Daniel 2:28). However, God doesn't merely *know* what's going to take place. He actually *causes* these things to occur.[1] In Scripture, God revealed His future plans to His prophets in nearly every book of the Bible. He did this through dreams, visions, appearances, and direct communication. Today, we have the completed revelation of God recorded in Scripture, which contains about 1,000 prophecies total. Of these, around 500 remain unfulfilled. So, more prophetic realities are coming. Clearly, our God is a God of prophecy!

#2 Why Should I Care About Bible Prophecy?

So, why is prophecy such a big deal? Why does God want us to know what He is going to do in the future? And how does this knowledge affect our lives right now. Here are seven compelling reasons why Bible prophecy is so important.

First, prophecy is in the Bible (2 Timothy 3:16-17). This may sound a bit obvious, but if God chose to include something in Scripture, then it must be there to teach us something about God, His plan for history, humanity, and for His children.

Second, prophecy makes up about 28 percent of the entire Bible. Remove prophecy from the Bible and you have essentially gutted a significant portion of Scripture's supernatural character. Consider:

- One out of every 30 verses in the New Testament contains prophecy.
- There are 8,000 total prophetic verses.
- Twenty-three out of 27 New Testament books mention the second coming of Jesus.
- For every time that the first coming of Jesus is mentioned, the second coming is mentioned *eight times*.
- The first prophecy concerning Christ is found in Genesis 3:15.
- There are 333 prophecies concerning Christ. Only 109 were fulfilled at His first coming. That leaves 224 prophecies yet to be fulfilled.

Third, according to Jesus, every word and letter of Scripture will eventually be fulfilled (Matthew 5:17-18). Every Old Testament prophecy about the Messiah was fulfilled—literally and exactly as Scripture predicted. Given this perfect track record, it stands to reason that every future prophecy will also be fulfilled in the same way. The Bible is batting 1.000 percent. It has never once gotten it wrong, but rather each prophecy so far has been fulfilled down to the most minute detail.[2]

Fourth, the last book of the Bible is 95 percent prophecy. God could have concluded His written revelation to man any way He wanted, and yet He chose to do so by giving us a heads-up on future history. Last words are lasting words. So, God must want us to know something about the future because His final word to us is *all about the future*!

ALL PREVIOUS PROPHECIES
WERE LITERALLY FULFILLED
SO
ALL FUTURE PROPHECIES
WILL BE LITERALLY FULFILLED

Fifth, prophecy is a big deal because God doesn't want His children to be uninformed regarding the end times (1 Thessalonians 4:13-18; 2 Thessalonians 2:1-5). But why? Because ignorance regarding prophecy can give rise to fear, anxiety, and uncertainty. It also makes us vulnerable to misleading information, false teachers, errant beliefs, sensationalism, speculation, conspiracy theories, and baseless predictions. Thankfully, our fears regarding the future can be conquered by reading God's prophetic word and trusting Him to accomplish it.

Sixth, prophecy is important because of the times we live in. At no time since Jesus walked the earth is end-times prophecy more likely to be fulfilled than it is right now. There is every indication to suggest that we are living in the last days. And since Revelation's realities could be just around the corner, the relevance of Bible prophecy has never been more real and relevant to Christians.

Finally, prophecy matters because of what it does for you and me. Bible prophecy gives us:

- Clarity (2 Thessalonians 2:1-5). Prophecy cuts through the fog, clears up the confusion, and enlightens us concerning what lies ahead.

- Confidence (2 Thessalonians 2:1-3). Once you can clearly see what's ahead, you can proceed with confidence and assurance.

You don't have to be timid about your beliefs concerning the rapture, the tribulation, the Antichrist, or Jesus' second coming. Prophecy imparts insight and wisdom, making you strong in your beliefs.

- Faith (Revelation 4). The *strength* of our faith is directly proportional to the *object* of our faith. If God is on His throne, guiding history toward its appointed end, then we can rest in knowing that not only does He hold the future, but us as well. Studying prophecy never breeds fear. It only builds faith.

- Hope (Titus 2:11-15; 1 Thessalonians 4:13). In Scripture, hope isn't a wish, but rather a *confident expectation*. Jesus' return for His bride is called the "blessed hope" (Titus 2:13). This hope fills us with expectation.[3] And that hope will not disappoint (Romans 5:3-5).

- Love for Jesus (Revelation 19:10). That's right. When you study Bible prophecy, it leads you straight to Jesus. That's because the ultimate point of prophecy is the Lord Jesus Christ. The more you study prophecy, the more you will be drawn into a closer and more intimate relationship with your Savior!

So, now you can see, God's prophetic plan for the future greatly impacts your life. That's why Bible prophecy is an essential part of our spiritual diet.

#3 Where in the Bible Do We Find Prophecy?

Of the 31,124 verses in the Bible, at least 8,352 of those contain prophecy (roughly 27 percent). Of those 8,352 prophetic verses, 6,312 have already been fulfilled. This leaves 2,040 verses that are modern-day and future endtime prophecies.[4] The first prophecy of the Bible is found in Genesis 2:17, and the last prophecy is found in Revelation 22:20. In between those two verses, prophecy is found throughout the Bible—occurring in single verses and in large continuous portions.

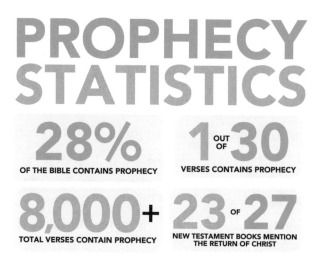

PROPHECY STATISTICS

28%
OF THE BIBLE CONTAINS PROPHECY

1 OUT OF 30
VERSES CONTAINS PROPHECY

8,000+
TOTAL VERSES CONTAIN PROPHECY

23 OF 27
NEW TESTAMENT BOOKS MENTION
THE RETURN OF CHRIST

Certain books—particularly the 16 books named after Old Testament prophets and the book of Revelation in the New Testament—are primarily focused on prophecy. For example, 8 of the 12 chapters of Daniel are prophetic in nature, and 18 of the 21 chapters in Revelation concern future prophecies about the tribulation period, the millennial kingdom, and the eternal state. A small number of books in the Bible—such as Esther and the Song of Solomon—do not contain any specific overt prophecies, but they contain prophetic types and figures linked to various prophetic themes and details.

Without question, the primary theme of prophecy is the coming of the Messiah. Genesis 3:15 prophesied that the seed of the woman (the virgin-born Savior) would one day crush the head of the serpent. From that verse to the end of Revelation, the key prophetic themes are primarily connected to the first and second advents of Jesus. There are over 300 prophecies about the first coming of Christ, and for every prophecy about the first coming of Christ, there are eight related to His second coming. In the Old Testament there are over 1,800 references to the return of Jesus. One out of every 30 verses in the New Testament is about the return of Christ. Of the 27 New Testament books, 23 give prominence to the second coming.

Prophecy is the backbone of the Bible. Every key person, theme, and line of theology connect directly to Bible prophecy. Fulfilled prophecy is the built-in verification system that proves the Bible is indeed the Word of God. God often points to prophecy as proof of His Word and His character. Fulfilled prophecy separates the Bible from any other religious work. One cannot study the pages of Scripture without bumping into prophecy.

#4 Are There Any Compelling Examples of Fulfilled Bible Prophecy?

Yes! The prophecies of the Bible are not vague or minor. The Bible is full of clear, compelling, detailed predictions of future events. Here are a few examples.

Messianic Prophecies

There are 109 separate and distinct prophecies (or over 300 if you include prophecies that are repeated in some form) about the Messiah that were fulfilled at Jesus' first coming. Specific details regarding the timing, conditions, lineage, and city of his birth, the nature of his life and ministry, and the specifics of his death, burial, and resurrection were all foretold long ago in the Old Testament Scriptures. Daniel chapter 9 foretold the exact timeframe for the first coming of Christ (to the day), and Isaiah 53 and Psalm 22 clearly depicted the crucifixion hundreds of years before the birth of Christ or the existence of the Roman Empire.

Prophecies About Major World Empires

In chapter 2 of the book of Daniel—written in the sixth century BC—the prophet, a Babylonian captive, interprets a vision of a statue for King Nebuchadnezzar, who had the dream. The statue in the dream had a head

GOLD

SILVER

BRONZE

IRON

IRON & CLAY

of gold, a chest and arms of silver, a belly and thighs of bronze, legs of iron, and feet and toes of iron mixed with clay.

Daniel explained that the first kingdom was Nebuchadnezzar's kingdom, the Babylonian kingdom—which would be followed by three other world kingdoms before it broke apart. This is exactly what happened.

From Daniel's time to our day, history records a succession of four increasingly larger empires symbolized by the metal that each was known for—Babylon, Medo-Persia, Greece, and Rome—and then a switch in format where the fourth empire eventually breaks down into an unstable mix (iron and clay) of nation-states with some strong and some weak. The final state of the empires will consist of ten toes, which represent ten powerful rulers during the tribulation period.

Prophecies About Israel and the Jewish People

Many prophecy experts call the rebirth of Israel in 1948 the super-sign. They refer to it this way mainly for two reasons. First, all other end-time signs hinge on this one sign. No other sign of the end could occur until Israel became a nation again. Second, experts call it the super-sign because of the sheer magnitude of this sign coming to pass. It is statistically impossible to predict this sign with all of its details and necessary preconditions, and have it fulfilled as it has in our modern era.

Jeremiah 16:14-15 reads, "Days are coming…when it will no longer be said, 'As the LORD lives, who brought up the sons of Israel out of the land of Egypt,' but, 'As the LORD lives, who brought up the sons of Israel from the land of the north and from all the countries where He had banished them.' For I will restore them to their own land which I gave to their fathers."

God proclaimed that when the dispersed Jewish people would return to their original homeland, this should be seen as a bigger miracle than the parting of the Red Sea! The dispersion of the Jewish people in AD 70, their mistreatment and preservation while scattered around the world, the desolation of the land of Israel during their absence, the return of the Jewish people to the very same land, the rebirth of Israel as a literal nation again, the ensuing attacks from border enemies, the growing financial and military strength of modern Israel, the global obsession with the tiny nation of Israel, and the exact geopolitical configuration of the Middle East right now were all foretold in great detail through various prophecies that are thousands of years old.

#5 How Do We Know Jesus Is Literally Returning to Earth?

The message of Christ's return has been on the lips of Jesus' bride for some 2,000 years. But how can we be sure His second coming will be an actual, *physical* appearance? Here are ten reasons to support such a belief:

1. Jesus' birth and existence were literal. This is attested to by religious as well as secular historians.[5] To allege otherwise is to make a baseless and ignorant claim.

2. Jesus' resurrection was literal, involving a physical body. When Christ rose from the dead, He possessed a physical body, though in a glorified state (1 Corinthians 15:44).[6]

3. Jesus promised to physically return at the end of the age (Matthew 16:27; 24:30-44; Luke 21:34-36; Revelation 19:11-16). There are over 300 references to this event in the New Testament.

4. The two angels at Jesus' ascension promised He would

physically return to the same spot (Acts 1:9-11). A physical ascension means a physical return.

5. Paul prophesied Jesus would be "*revealed* from heaven with His mighty angels" (2 Thessalonians 1:7).[7] Clearly literal, not symbolic, language.

6. His return will be *visible*, and "every eye will see Him" (Revelation 1:7; Matthew 24:27-30; 26:64).

7. Specific geographical locations are associated with His coming: Armageddon (Revelation 16:16), the Mount of Olives (Zechariah 14:3-4; Acts 1:9-11), and Jerusalem (Zechariah 12:1-3; 14:2; Revelation 16:17-21).

8. Actual global armies will assemble to do battle at Armageddon against the coming Christ (Revelation 19:19-21). Jesus and His armies ride white horses (Revelation 19:11,14).

9. The second coming of Jesus ushers in a literal thousand-year millennial kingdom (Revelation 19–20).

10. Jesus' literal return is based on a literal approach to all Scripture, including Revelation. The early church held to this interpretation and expected any day to see Jesus return for them.[8]

> **All previous prophecies were literally fulfilled, meaning all future ones will also be literally fulfilled.**

The second coming of Jesus Christ is the climax of Revelation's prophetic narrative. And by all indications, the Bible prophesies a literal, future, physical return of our Lord.

#6 How Can Bible Prophecy Help Convince Skeptics and Unbelievers?

When it comes to Scripture's credibility, nothing is more compelling and convincing than fulfilled prophecy. Keep in mind, every Christian is an apologist, not just pastors and "professionals" (Jude 3; 1 Peter 3:15). Even so, none of us has the ability to convince an unwilling skeptic or a closed-minded unbeliever. But thankfully, God delights in using His Word through people like us to lead others to salvation (2 Corinthians 5:11).

Here are four reasons why Bible prophecy can be a powerful apologetic.

First, the Bible is batting a thousand when it comes to fulfilled prophecy. It has never missed or been off in the slightest manner, but rather always comes true exactly as God predicted. Every prophecy concerning the Messiah's first coming was fulfilled, literally and precisely, as recorded in the Old Testament. If just *one* of those prophecies had turned out to be false or unfulfilled, we would have reason to question the Bible's authenticity. Therefore, since previous prophecies came true, we can expect all subsequent prophecies to do the same.

Second, fulfilled prophecy is strong evidence of the Bible's divine authorship, for only God can predict the future hundreds and thousands of years before it occurs.[9] Here are some of the over 100 prophecies Jesus fulfilled at His first coming:

- He would be born to a virgin.[10]
- His physical place of birth was named.[11]

- He would ride into Jerusalem on a donkey.[12]

- He would be beaten and abused.[13]

- He would be betrayed with money.[14]

- His hands and feet would be pierced.[15]

- He would die with criminals.[16]

- His bones would not be broken.[17]

- Though killed with wicked men, His grave would be associated with a rich man.[18]

- He would be physically raised from the dead.[19]

The odds of one person fulfilling *just eight* of those prophecies is 1 in 1,000,000,000,000,000! Or one in one *quadrillion*.[20]

Third, since the Bible is accurate regarding all these fulfilled prophecies, it stands to reason that it can be trusted in other areas as well: science, history, morality, marriage and family, sexuality, relationships, and how to live (2 Timothy 3:16-17; 2 Peter 1:2-4).

Fourth, we are currently witnessing many of Revelation's future prophecies in their embryonic and developmental forms. These are so blatantly obvious that they rise far above the category of mere coincidence.

Because of the Bible's impeccable track record, Jesus' second coming, along with the hundreds of other end-times prophecies as of yet unfulfilled, are *preauthenticated* and *guaranteed* to occur, with 100 percent certainty.

Of course, facts alone are not sufficient to change a person's mind and to convince them to trust Christ. God's miraculous power through the Holy Spirit must also draw people to Jesus, convicting them of their sin and of their need for a Savior (John 6:44,65; 16:7-11).

Scripture says in the last days many will scoff at Bible prophecy (2 Peter 3:3-9). But this only highlights all the more our need for prophecy apologetics.

Have you ever been in a dark room, and then gradually brightened the lights, giving your eyes time to adjust to it? If so, then you understand a bit of how God revealed the Bible to His people. Beginning with basic truths, He incrementally added to His revelation over the course of some 1,500 years. Theologians call this progressive revelation, meaning God's truth came to us not all at once but in installments.

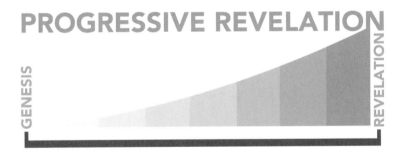

Bible prophecy was also given this way. Each prophet received only a portion of what was to be revealed and fulfilled later on. Adam and Eve did not know what Moses knew. And Moses did not know what Isaiah knew. And Isaiah did not know what John the Baptist knew. John the Baptist did not know what Paul knew. And Paul did not know everything that John would know from Jesus' revelation to him.

Throughout the Old and New Testaments, God required a specific level of obedience corresponding to the revelation that had been given thus far. The basis of salvation and forgiveness of sin has always been the same from Adam until now—the shed blood of a substitutionary sacrifice, symbolized and foreshadowed through bulls and goats in the Old Testament, and ultimately made by Jesus Christ. However, the content of believers' faith differed and progressed from age to age, depending upon the extent of God's revelation. Some theologians refer to these ages as dispensations or stewardships. In each era of stewardship, believers were required to live up to the light of revelation that had been given to them.

This principle of stewardship also applies when it comes to Bible prophecy. The prophet Micah knew the name of Messiah's birthplace (Micah 5:2), but he did not know about Antichrist's future kingdom (Daniel 2 and 7). Paul wrote of the blessed hope of the rapture (1 Thessalonians 4:13-18) but was not given revelation to write about the seal, bowl, and trumpet judgments (Revelation 6–19).[21]

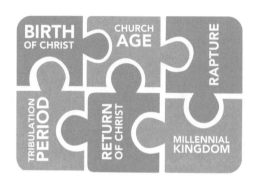

Of course, now that the Bible has been written and God's revelation is complete, we have the privilege of seeing all Scripture's prophecies. We have all the pieces of the puzzle on the table, and proper Bible study methods along with the guidance and illumination of the Holy Spirit allow us to understand Scripture's message. And because of that completed revelation, ours is the most accountable generation since the beginning of creation. Being obedient to what God has given us through prophecy is more important now in these last days than ever before.

#8 Who Were the Prophets?

There was (roughly) a 300-year period in Israel's ancient history when several prophets were sent to call the Jewish people to turn back to the Lord. They recorded the prophecies in books bearing their names. The books of the prophets are broken down into two categories—the major prophets and the minor prophets. This doesn't mean some were more important than others, but that the major prophets wrote larger books than the minor prophets.

The prophets recorded prophecies about their day as well as many prophecies about the end times. This is known as the mountain peaks of Bible prophecy. As the prophets foretold the future, they would often shift back and forth between immediate events and end-time events. They didn't always know how much time was in between the mountain peaks. They just recorded what they were told and many times didn't know what their prophecies were all about. For example, on more than one occasion Daniel stated his confusion about some prophecies and was told that some prophecies were rolled up and sealed until the time of the end (Daniel 12:4,8-9).

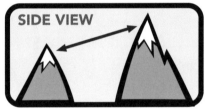

By the time of the prophets, the country had split into two with Israel being the north and Judah to the south. Some prophets were in Israel and some in Judah. Others, such as Daniel, were in captivity away from their country. The major prophets were Isaiah, Jeremiah, Ezekiel, and Daniel. The minor prophets were Hosea, Joel, Amos, Obadiah, Jonah, Micah, Nahum, Habakkuk, Zephaniah, Haggai, Zechariah, and Malachi.

In addition to these well-known figures, there were many other prophets in the Bible, such as Elijah and Elisha. Peter and Paul were prophets in the sense that they foretold future events. So was Jude. The most famous prophet of the New Testament is John. He was Jesus' closest disciple and he wrote the book of Revelation—the most prophetic (and final) book of the New Testament.

#9 Are Any Prophecies Being Fulfilled in Our Day?

The rebirth of Israel in 1948 was definitely a fulfillment of prophecy (Isaiah 66:8) and began to set the stage for all of the remaining end-time prophecies to be fulfilled. Other prophecies related to Israel and the Jewish people are being fulfilled in our day. For example, the Bible predicted that the Jewish people would return to Israel from all over the world (Isaiah 43:5-6; Jeremiah 16:14-15; Ezekiel 36:22-24). Over the past 120+ years, more than 3.5 million Jewish people have changed their citizenship and immigrated to Israel from all over the world. This prophecy continues to be fulfilled as tens of thousands of Jewish people each year return to their ancient homeland.

Scripture also predicted that Israel's land would be a wasteland for a long period but would become fruitful once her people returned (Ezekiel 36:33-36; 38:8), that Israel would become a wealthy and prosperous nation (Jeremiah 31:23; Ezekiel 38:10-13), that she would once again be in control of Jerusalem (Zechariah 8:4-8; Luke 21:24), that she would have great military strength (Zechariah 12:6), and that the nations of the world would be obsessed with Israel and her borders (Zechariah 12:2-3). All of these prophecies have been—and continue to be—fulfilled in our day. They are necessary for all the future prophecies related to the millennial kingdom to be fulfilled.

We are also witnessing the predicted apostasy of the church (1 Timothy 4:1-3; 2 Timothy 4:3-4; Revelation 3:14-22), the prophesied increase in travel and knowledge (Daniel 12:4), the lawlessness Jesus spoke of (Matthew 24:12), and all of the end-time characteristics Paul spoke of in 2 Timothy 3:1-5, where we read,

> But realize this, that in the last days difficult times will come.
> For men will be lovers of self, lovers of money, boastful, arrogant, revilers, disobedient to parents, ungrateful, unholy, unloving, irreconcilable, malicious gossips, without self-control, brutal, haters of good, treacherous, reckless, conceited lovers of

pleasure rather than lovers of God, holding to a form of godliness, although they have denied its power; avoid such men as these.

In addition to those specific prophecies being fulfilled in modern times, there are also several prophetic end-time conditions related to the church and Gentile (non-Jewish) nations that are very clearly forming in our day.

It has been said that the closer we get to the future tribulation period, the more its shadows will be cast on the church age. Prophecy doesn't happen in a vacuum, and as we approach the end of the church age, we should expect to see conditions trending in a specific way—and we do.

TRIBULATION PERIOD CASTING ITS SHADOW

#10 How Should Christians Live if Jesus Might Return Any Day Now?

The reality of the rapture is a positive gamechanger for our lives in many ways. But this is where we may encounter some tension as well. For if Jesus really could come back today, should we still be going about our lives like we always do? Or should we instead focus only on the "spiritual stuff"?

Waiting for Christ to return does not mean we should sell all our possessions, climb the nearest mountain, and meditate until He comes. Every New Testament believer knew Jesus could return at any time to rescue His bride. And yet, there is every indication they continued on with their daily lives. Jesus, Paul, John, and Peter all urge us to be faithful to the Lord, penetrate the darkness, and live a convincing life apologetic.

With that in mind, here are four principles that will help us toward this goal.

Perspective: This World Is Not My Home

Though we remain here on the earth right now, our citizenship is actually in heaven (Philippians 3:20). Our home is with Him. Remaining here means we live for Christ and to die is great gain (Galatians 2:20; Philippians 1:21). It's a win-win proposition.

Our time here on the earth is temporary, but that doesn't mean it's unimportant. The way we presently live will impact our future rewards in heaven (1 Corinthians 3:10-15; 2 Corinthians 5:9-10). We maintain both an earthly and an eternal perspective. Our future influences our present. This perspective gives us hope and encouragement.

Penetration: I Must Shine Christ's Light in a Dark World

It's no secret that we're living in evil days (Ephesians 5:16). Jesus' generation was no different, which is why He told His disciples to be a light for Him (Matthew 5:14-16).

If Jesus wanted His bride to be in heaven right now, that's exactly where she would be. You may live an extended lifetime here, or you could be called home tomorrow. But no matter how long our lives, we must shine His light for the duration.

This involves being obedient and faithful to God in the daily, ordinary tasks He has called us to. Jesus doesn't ask us to abandon life's daily duties in order to be preoccupied with His return. So, whether He comes on this day or ten years from now, we persevere till the end.

Preparation: I Need to Make Myself Ready to Meet the Lord

John wrote, "We know that when He appears, we will be like Him, because we will see Him just as He is. And everyone who has this hope fixed on Him purifies himself, just as He is pure" (1 John 3:2-3). A bride's greatest desire is to be ready and prepared for her wedding day and her husband. Christ's promised return does the same thing for us. It puts purpose and passion into our daily lives, motivating and preparing us to meet Him (2 Peter 3:11-13).

Priorities: God Must Remain #1 in My Life

Jesus declared that our love for Him must far outweigh all other earthly relationships, even the love of our own lives (Luke 14:25-35). Loving the world and the things in it causes us to slide into spiritual mediocrity and lukewarmness (James 4:4; 1 John 2:15-17; Revelation 3:14-16). But when God is our number one priority, those other priorities take care of themselves (Psalm 37:4; Matthew 6:33). We are free to love Him, live our lives to the fullest, and simultaneously long for our Savior's return!

CHAPTER 2

THE DIFFERENT VIEWS

#1 Should We Avoid Teaching Certain Prophecies Because People Have Different Views?

Ever wondered why there are so many views when it comes to the end times, and why there is such division and disagreement among scholars and godly men? Given that this disagreement exists, does that mean one's view of the end times is unimportant, perhaps even optional? Is it really necessary that we have a specific view of Jesus' return, the rapture, the millennial kingdom? Or should we leave our options open and just let God sort it out?

Let's begin by exploring some of the reasons why we avoid teaching or talking about the subject in church or with our Christian friends.

- We want to preserve unity. We think that if we discuss it, we might get into an argument. And arguing alienates and divides us instead of bringing us together.

- We don't want to offend anyone. Before social media, we didn't have near as much contact and exposure to Christians from diverse backgrounds, beliefs, and denominations. But all that's changed now. Make one wrong post and you risk offending hundreds of your brothers and sisters.

- We don't want to be perceived as proud or self-righteous because we believe our view is the right one. We should pursue humility and not portray pride, so not sharing our view will potentially help avoid this.

- We don't know enough yet and are therefore not confident enough to discuss it. Even many pastors have not educated themselves enough to be able to teach effectively on the subject.

- We think it is not possible for anyone to know the right view. We live in a world where everyone *except* Christians can be right. And yet, only one view of the end times can be correct, since each one mutually excludes the others.

Because God has given us so much information about these prophetic events in His Word, they must be very important to Him...and therefore should be to us as well. Since all Scripture is profitable, the teaching concerning the last days and Christ's return is by no means a minor or marginal topic.

Second, to say one's view of eschatology (or any doctrine) is unimportant just because there is disagreement about it is to devalue not only the doctrine but the very Word of God itself. There are many important teachings in the Bible about which there have been enormous debates and disagreements over the centuries, but this fact doesn't in any way diminish the importance of those doctrines. Instead of avoiding it because there are different views, why not study all the views and discover how others have come to their respective conclusions?

#2 What Are the Four Interpretation Methods?

How do people form their beliefs concerning end-times prophecy? And which views make the most sense biblically? An important principle to keep in mind is that your belief regarding the end times is determined by your approach to Scripture. Interpreting the Bible (called the study of hermeneutics) is a discipline that carries serious implications. *Your approach always determines your destination.*

For example, when a plane is approaching a runway, the pilot must properly line up the plane or it will miss the runway altogether. He must preset his coordinates, then make sure he stays on course the entire way. If his flight path is off at the beginning of his journey (and he never course corrects), then he will miss the runway, the airport, and even his destination city! The same is true with interpreting the Bible and prophecy. How you begin will determine how you will end up. If you begin with a flawed approach, you will certainly miss the "runway" (i.e., the meaning of the passage).

Interpreting Bible prophecy through numerology, Jewish feasts, current events, natural catastrophes, or visions and dreams are all highly subjective, unreliable, and inaccurate methods. Instead, here are some time-tested, reliable principles for helping you understand the Bible and its prophetic sections:

BIBLE INTERPRETATION

ME

Interpret Scripture Literally

Traditionally, there have been two general methods or approaches to studying the end times: the literal and the symbolic or allegorical methods. The literal approach takes a biblical passage at face value, assuming it says what it means and means what it says. A good rule of Bible study is, "When the plain sense of Scripture makes common sense, seek no other sense…lest you end up with *nonsense*!"[22]

By contrast, the allegorical approach sees Scripture's words as pointing to something else, usually some deeper spiritual meaning. The literal approach will lead you to specific views regarding Revelation and the end times, while the allegorical approach will lead you to a multitude of views.

So, when studying your Bible, ask, "What is the normal, plain understanding of the passage in its original context? What is happening with grammar, verb tense, word choice, historical settings, and cultural customs of the day?"

FIGURATIVE/INCONSISTENT

ALREADY HAPPENED
PRETERIST

OVERVIEW OF CHURCH HISTORY
HISTORICIST

JUST ALLEGORY
SYMBOLIC

LITERAL FULFILLMENT
FUTURIST

Recognize Symbolic Language

There *are* symbols in the Bible and in Bible prophecy, where we see riders on horses, beasts, serpents, bowls, horns, stars, and many other symbols. However, all these word pictures point to literal truths. Always. A symbol is a word or phrase that represents something other than itself. And Revelation, for example, is full of symbols that are explained in either the immediate context or some other place in the book (Revelation 11:8; 12:1-6; 17:1-18). So don't be alarmed when you encounter symbols, but look for how the passage or context explains it. And remember, you cannot make up your own meaning of the symbol.

Let Scripture Interpret Scripture

Because we know that all Scripture is inspired by God, we know the Bible will not contradict itself but will often clarify itself elsewhere. It's like putting together pieces of the puzzle to form a unified picture. If we knew only what a single passage says about Jesus, faith, or the Antichrist, then our knowledge would be limited and incomplete. But by cross-referencing and doing some Bible study, we can get the full picture.

See the Mountain Peaks and Valleys

This is especially true when it comes to prophecy. No one of God's prophets was given complete revelation concerning the coming Messiah. Isaiah and Micah are given information regarding His birth, but Isaiah also knew about the suffering of the Messiah. Daniel saw the activities of the Antichrist, and he, Isaiah, Micah, and Haggai all received information regarding Messiah's future kingdom. But no one got the full story. They saw some of the mountain peaks but not all the valleys (or information that would help them fill in the blanks). One of those valleys was the mystery of the church, which none of the prophets knew about (Romans 16:25-26; Ephesians 3:1-7). But with the completion of God's written revelation, we now know all the details concerning the Messiah's first coming and much about His second coming.

#3 What Are the Three Main Views About the Timing of the Rapture?

There are several beliefs concerning the blessed hope (rapture), and all have to do with its *timing*. Virtually all Christian traditions and denominations believe Christ will return. However, *when* Jesus rescues His bride carries with it some pretty serious implications.

The *pretribulation view* says that Christ will return *prior* to the time of tribulation described in Revelation 6 through 19. This event is not what officially begins the tribulation period. The signing of Antichrist's covenant with Israel is (Daniel 9:27). In this view, believers will not suffer during the tribulation because they won't be there. God has promised to rescue us from the wrath to come (1 Thessalonians 5:9-10) and to deliver us from "the hour of testing, that hour which is about to come upon the whole world, to test those who dwell on the earth" (Revelation 3:10).

The *midtribulation view* claims Jesus will return at the *halfway point* of the seven-year tribulation. This halfway point represents the separation between the tribulation and the great tribulation. Here, His return coincides with Antichrist's invasion of the Jewish temple and the enforcement of the "mark of the beast" (Revelation 12–13). This view believes the seal judgments (Revelation 6) are not God's wrath but rather come from man. So, Christians will suffer three-and-a-half years of persecution. One of the issues with this view is that it removes the doctrine of imminence regarding Jesus' return. Imminence means Christ can return at any time. Knowing that He returns three-and-a-half years after the tribulation begins removes imminence, as we would be able to predict the timing of His coming.

The *posttribulation view* believes Christians will endure *all* of the tribulation and its horrific judgments. They will suffer and be persecuted, after

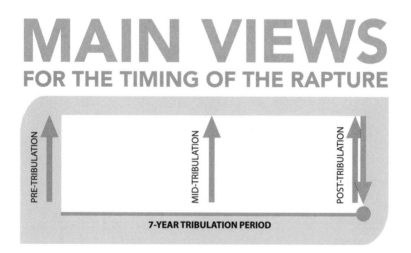

MAIN VIEWS
FOR THE TIMING OF THE RAPTURE

PRE-TRIBULATION

MID-TRIBULATION

POST-TRIBULATION

7-YEAR TRIBULATION PERIOD

which they will be rescued *just before* Christ returns at His second coming (Armageddon). Those who believe this view justify it partially from Jesus' words about persecution during the tribulation in Matthew 24 and from His teaching on being hated by the world in John 15. The posttribulation view also removes imminence, since it occurs exactly at the endpoint of the seven-year period of time.

There is a fourth view, known as the *prewrath view*, which sees the rapture taking place about five-and-a-half years into the tribulation. Believers are rescued, this view claims, when the sixth seal is opened (Revelation 6:12) and God's wrath begins to be poured out. An obscure fifth view says that only certain believers are taken in the rapture, while others who have been disobedient are left behind to endure the tribulation. Hardly any serious Bible student believes in this *partial rapture* theory.

#4 What Are the Three Views of the Millennium?

As you might expect, there are also multiple interpretations concerning Jesus' millennial reign. And again, all of them hinge upon one's interpretive approach to Scripture (literal or symbolic).

Amillennialism. This view says Christ's thousand-year reign (the millennium) is only a *symbol* of Christ's rule throughout the entire church age, at the end of which He will return at His second coming. Typically, amillennialists must spiritualize virtually all the events of the tribulation in order to reach their conclusions. Some amillennialists are also preterists, believing parts of Revelation (symbolically or literally) occurred in the first century.[23]

Postmillennialism. Those who hold this view must also spiritualize Revelation, as they see the church age as Christ's millennial reign. They believe the church will essentially usher in the second coming of Christ through making the world more and more Christianized. Unfortunately, history and our current age of sin and apostasy do not lend credibility to this view.

Premillennialism. Premillennialists see a literal thousand-year reign of

Christ upon the earth, preceded by seven years of tribulation and His second coming at Armageddon. If you read Revelation at face value, no one could claim the seal, trumpet, and bowl judgments have previously occurred the way they are described in Scripture or at any point in the last 2,000 years. Premillennialism interprets many of God's promises to Abraham and David as unconditional, literal, and (presently) future. Christ will reign from David's throne "forever" as previously promised, and Israel will enjoy the full land boundaries originally pledged to them by God (Genesis 12:1; 15:18-21; 2 Samuel 7:12-16; 1 Kings 4:21). In this view, Jesus is not currently reigning from David's throne; He is sitting at the right hand of the throne of God (Hebrews 12:2). However, when He returns at the end of the tribulation, He will take His place on this promised throne (Acts 15:15-18).

Because Jesus' first and second comings are literal, physical, and to the earth, so will be His future millennial reign. Premillennialism was the dominant belief of the early church and for the first three centuries after Pentecost. Also, John is directed to use the number 1,000 six times in seven verses

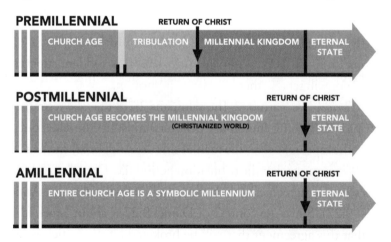

THE THREE VIEWS
OF THE MILLENNIUM

PREMILLENNIAL   RETURN OF CHRIST

CHURCH AGE | TRIBULATION | MILLENNIAL KINGDOM | ETERNAL STATE

POSTMILLENNIAL   RETURN OF CHRIST

CHURCH AGE BECOMES THE MILLENNIAL KINGDOM (CHRISTIANIZED WORLD) | ETERNAL STATE

AMILLENNIAL   RETURN OF CHRIST

ENTIRE CHURCH AGE IS A SYMBOLIC MILLENNIUM | ETERNAL STATE

(Revelation 20:1-7). If that number isn't literal, then why would God repeat that specific number over and over again? Why not simply say "a very long time," or employ some sort of clearly symbolic language? For those reasons and more, we believe that Jesus will reign on the earth for 1,000 actual years.

#5 In What Basic Order Will the End Times Unfold?

Several key passages of Scripture harmonize to logically piece together a clear order of events.

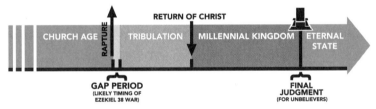

The Rapture. The rapture is a sign-less, imminent (could happen at any moment) future event when all believers will be transformed and taken instantly to meet Jesus in the air and then into heaven (John 14:2-3; 1 Corinthians 15:51-52; 1 Thessalonians 4:15-18). This sudden, supernatural, global event will set all other key events in motion.

Gap Period. We learn in 2 Thessalonians 2:7-8 that the restrainer (the Holy Spirit indwelling church-age believers) must first be taken out of the way (via the rapture) before the man of sin (the Antichrist) can be revealed. Daniel 9 informs us that the tribulation period (i.e. Daniel's "70th Week") begins when an agreement "with the many" is finalized by the Antichrist (Daniel 9:27). Since the context of Daniel 9:27 is about Israel, it makes sense that this agreement that will be brokered by the Antichrist will be between Israel and "the many." Logic demands a presumably short gap period before the tribulation.

Ezekiel 38 War. This prophecy foretells a specific end-time attack on Israel from the north. We believe this will be a post-rapture power grab led by Russia in partnership with Iran and Turkey and others (see Ezekiel 38–39). Experts vary on how this war fits into the order of events and whether or not a Psalm 83 war must occur first.

The Beginning of the Tribulation Period. In the chaotic aftermath of the rapture, a world leader will rise to power and broker a deal between Israel and "many" (Daniel 9:27), officially beginning the seven-year tribulation period.

The Midpoint of the Tribulation Period. The Antichrist will break his covenant with Israel at the exact midpoint of the seven-year period (Daniel 9:27), defile the temple, and turn against the Jewish people. A remnant of the Jewish people will be protected and will turn to Christ as Savior at the end of the tribulation period (Daniel 12:1-2; Matthew 23:39; Romans 11:25-27; Revelation 12:13-17; 14:1-5).

The Return of Christ. At the end of the tribulation period Jesus will physically return to earth's surface with the armies of heaven (angels and church-age believers) following behind Him (Revelation 19:11-21).

The Millennial Kingdom. The Old Testament contains many prophecies of a yet-future golden era when a descendant of David will rule the entire world from Jerusalem. This thousand-year period (Revelation 20:1-6) will follow the tribulation (with a short time period to transition to the kingdom age). Satan will be released at the end for one final battle. He will be quickly defeated and thrown permanently into the lake of fire (Revelation 20:7-10).

The Great White Throne Judgment. All nonbelievers throughout history will stand before God to be judged and, sadly, cast into the lake of fire. Believers will not stand before God at this judgment because their sins have been covered by the atonement of Jesus (Revelation 20:11-15).

The New Heaven and New Earth. All creation will be completely reno-vated or recreated. The center of activity and God's presence will be in the new Jerusalem, but presumably we will be able to spend eternity traveling the vast areas of heaven.

#6 What Was Taught About Eschatology in the New Testament?

Eschatology plays a prominent role in both the Old and New Testaments. The return of Christ is not a fringe or secondary topic in the New Tes-tament—rather it is a foundational pillar of New Testament teaching. Twenty-three of the 27 New Testament books give prominence to the topic of Christ's return, and all but two of the smaller epistles contain prophecy. Of the 260 chapters in the New Testament, there are more than 300 refer-ences to this all-important future event. One out of every 30 verses in the New Testament discusses the subject of Christ's return.

Jesus' second longest recorded teaching is on the topic of the end times (second only to the Sermon on the Mount). Matthew, Mark, and Luke all record this teaching—known as the Olivet Discourse (Matthew 24–25; Mark 13; Luke 21). Paul recorded intricate details of the rapture (1 Corin-thians 15:51-53; 1 Thessalonians 4:13-18), along with key details about the future Antichrist and the tribulation period. Peter and Jude both highlight aspects of end-time events, and, of course, John provides the largest amount of eschatological detail of all in the final book of the Bible—Revelation.

According to J. Barton Payne's *Encyclopedia of Biblical Prophecy*, every book in the New Testament except Philemon and 3 John contains proph-ecy about future events, including the return of the Lord. Here is a chart highlighting the amount of prophecy found in each of the 27 New Testa-ment books.[24]

ESCHATOLOGY[4]
IN THE NEW TESTAMENT

BOOK	# OF PROPHECIES	# OF VERSES	% OF BOOK
Matthew	81	278	26%
Mark	50	125	19%
Luke	75	250	22%
John	45	180	20%
Acts	63	125	13%
Romans	29	91	21%
1 Corinthians	25	85	19%
2 Corinthians	7	12	5%
Galatians	7	16	11%
Ephesians	7	8	5%
Philippians	5	10	10%
Colossians	4	9	9%
1 Thess	9	16	18%
2 Thess	12	19	40%
1 Timothy	2	5	4%
2 Timothy	8	17	20%
Titus	1	1	2%
Philemon	0	0	0%
Hebrews	52	147	45%
James	4	7	6%
1 Peter	11	21	20%
2 Peter	11	25	41%
1 John	4	6	6%
2 John	2	2	15%
3 John	0	0	0%
Jude	8	10	40%
Revelation	56	256	63%

What Was Taught About Eschatology in the Early Church?

The early church was focused primarily on spreading the good news about the Messiah's resurrection and offer of salvation to anyone who would receive Him. It was also focused on survival as persecution ramped up in the late first century and continued until the early fourth century.

The final book of the New Testament was written around AD 95. During the first century, Christians readily accepted the writings of the apostles as authoritative. Between AD 110 and the early fourth century (about the

CANONIZATION PROCESS
HOW THE BOOKS OF THE BIBLE WERE COMPILED

c. AD 35-95	New Testament books immediately accepted by Christians (2 Pet 3:16; 1 Tim 5:18). The later acceptance of a canon was for official recognition as the church grew and spread.
c. AD 110	Every book of the NT cited (except two) by Ignatius, Clement of Rome, and Polycarp. By AD 150, the apostolic fathers cited every NT book as authoritative.
c. AD 140	The first attempt at a canon was by the heretic Marcion, who rejected the entire OT and only accepted most of Paul's letters and Luke as Scripture.
c. AD 200	Muratorian Canon—L.A. Muratori discovered a canon list in the Milan Library that included the Synoptic Gospels, Pauline epistles, 1 & 2 John, Jude, and Revelation.
EARLY 300s	The Apostolic Canon 85 (final Latin version) accepts all books of the Old and New Testaments except Revelation.
AD 325	Eusebius lists all the Gospels, Pauline epistles (not Philemon), 1 Peter, 1 John, and Revelation of John. He does not list the general epistles, 2 Peter, 2 & 3 John, and Jude.
MID-300s	Theodor Mommsen discovered a 10th-century Latin list (published 1886) that contains all New Testament books except six. The list probably originated in North Africa by the 4th century. This is known as the Cheltenham Canon.
AD 367	Athanasius, Bishop of Alexandria, lists all 27 books in his paschal letter. This is the earliest complete canon of the New Testament.
AD 382/397	The Synod of Rome (382) gave final approval of the canon for all the Western churches. The Synod of Carthage (397) gave final acceptance of the canon to the entire church. Thus, the canon is complete.

time when the great Roman persecutions subsided) various church fathers (Ignatius, Clement of Rome, Polycarp, and others) grouped New Testament writings with some slight variation. Later in the fourth century (AD 367) Athanasius, Bishop of Alexandria, lists all 27 books of the New Testament and by the end of the fourth century (AD 382–397) the canon of the 27 writings was completely settled.

During this early period when the church was just getting grounded and focused on sharing the gospel, there was really no systematic study of eschatology. Because of this, the early church commonly held contradictory positions without really being aware of this fact. During this early period we find evidence of both the pretribulation view of the rapture and the posttribulation view of the rapture.

Imminency (the idea that the rapture could occur at any moment) was taught by early church fathers such as Clement of Rome, Ignatius of Antioch, and several others. The Shepherd of Hermas (around AD 140–154) even taught the concept of escaping the future tribulation period.

So, though not formalized in a systematic fashion, the concept of a pretribulational rapture existed, and was the broadly accepted view in the earliest church period following the deaths of the apostles.

#8 What Was Taught About Eschatology in the Dark Ages?

An interpretation method known to us today as *the idealist view* teaches that all prophecy about the end times is merely figurative. This view is also sometimes referred to as *the spiritual view*. This is because it allegorizes (or spiritualizes) prophetic texts, particularly as it pertains to the book of Revelation and end-time events.

This interpretation method leads to a position known as amillennialism (the idea that the future kingdom age spoken of in Scripture is only figurative). The idealist interpretation method holds that the seven-year tribulation period is merely figurative as well, and that the rapture and return of the Lord at the end of the age are rolled into one single event.

This school of thought arose around AD 190 from the area of Alexandria, Egypt, and was adopted by the fourth-century theologian Augustine of Hippo. Augustine applied this spiritualization only to prophetic texts, unlike the Alexandrians, who applied it to most or all of Scripture. Augustine's teaching gained a following and eventually became the dominant view of the Roman Catholic Church beginning in the fourth century.

From the fifth century to sixteenth century—the entire medieval period—this allegorized view of prophecy was the official protected position of the church. Any dissenting views were considered heretical. Many people were burned at the stake or otherwise killed for teaching doctrine that did not line up with the official Roman Catholic views. Any writings that taught other views (if found) were likewise destroyed.

Therefore, we really do not know how many Christians during the Dark Ages used the literal interpretation method that the early church held (and that the New Testament clearly teaches). Because of this we can't really determine how many Christians during the medieval period held the pretribulation view of eschatology.

It is very probable that some form of premillennialism existed during the Middle Ages—presumably underground. Many have suspected that the Albigenses, Lombards, and Waldenses leaned toward the premillennial view,[25] but like many works alluded to above, their written works were destroyed. In 1304, a man known as Brother Dolcino taught a form of the pretribulation view.[26]

The main concern with interpretation methods (and the various end-time views they result in) is whether or not they are biblical. The key questions to ask are: Does it square with Scripture? Is it consistent with God's character and past history? Does it allow for the same interpretation method to be used from Genesis to Revelation?

The literal futurist view (that future prophecy is literally future prophecy), along with the resulting conclusion that the future tribulation period is a literal period of God's wrath that sets up a literal future millennial

kingdom, is scripturally sound and seems to have had proponents throughout church history, including during the Dark Ages.

END-TIME VIEWS
IN CHURCH HISTORY

1st century: early church taught pretrib/premil view

3rd century: allegorical view of Scripture crept in

4th century: amil view dominant in Catholic Church

4th century-1517: no other dominant views allowed/encouraged

1600s-1700s: Puritans and others interpret Scripture literally

1800s: Darby and others revive and expound the pretrib/premil view

1900s: Scofield, Ironside, Walvoord advance the pretrib/premil view

Late 1900s: popular books educate lay people
    1970 *The Late Great Planet Earth* (Hal Lindsey)
    1995-2007 *The Left Behind Series* (Tim LaHaye)

#9 What Was Taught About Eschatology from the Reformation to Today?

Key figures of the Protestant Reformation, such as Martin Luther and John
Calvin, did a great service to Christians everywhere by reforming many of
the teachings of the established church—primarily the doctrine of salvation by grace through faith alone, but also the other key *solas*.

Unfortunately, the reformers didn't go far enough. While they helped
people return to a clear, literal interpretation of Scripture as it pertained to
the doctrine of salvation, they did not apply this literal interpretation to
the events surrounding the return of Christ.

When it came to eschatology, the reformers maintained the allegorized
view of prophecy—along with the idea that the tribulation period and the
future kingdom were merely allegory. The reformers viewed the book of

THE FIVE SOLAS

Sola Scriptura	"Scripture alone"
Sola Fide	"faith alone"
Sola Gratia	"grace alone"
Solus Christus	"Christ alone"
Soli Deo Gloria	"to the glory of God alone"

Revelation as a symbolic overview of church history, and they connected the Catholic Church with all of the negative symbolism in the book.

In response to this, Catholic theologians developed what is known as *the preterist view* in an attempt to sway popular belief away from post-Reformation teaching. The preterist view teaches that the events of Revelation had already occurred in the first century when Rome destroyed Jerusalem in AD 70. The preterist view is still the primary view of Roman Catholics, and it has been carried over into some Protestant denominations as well.

If the allegorical view was developed because Christ's second coming seemed to be taking too long, then the preterist view was developed to shift negative focus away from the post-Reformation Catholic Church. Neither of these were godly motives. God's Word can be taken at face value and trusted implicitly. God says what He means and means what He says (Psalm 19:7; John 1:1; 2 Timothy 3:16; 2 Peter 1:19-21; Revelation 22:18-19).

As more and more lay people had access to the Bible in their own language, groups such as the Puritans (in the 1600s) returned to a literal interpretation of Scripture, leading them to view yet-unfulfilled Bible prophecy as literal future events. This became known as *the futurist interpretation method*. Rather than allegorizing tough prophecies to fit their ideas, they taught that the church could look forward to literal end-time events—including a rebirth of the nation of Israel.

Using the literal interpretation method, in 1830, John Darby systematized and helped popularize the pretribulation view of the rapture. Some have argued that this was the first time the church taught the pretribulation view, but as you can see from the history of the early and medieval churches (detailed in the previous chapters), this argument is simply not true.

All four views (idealist, historicist, preterist, futurist) found pockets in various denominations and geographical areas. In the 1900s, a handful of American theologians, including Harry Ironside and Charles Ryrie, further systematized and popularized the pretribulation view in a few key seminaries. The pretribulation view became the dominant view in America among evangelical Christians, including the majority of Baptists, Presbyterians, and charismatics.

In 1970, during the early years of the Jesus movement, Hal Lindsey's book *The Late Great Planet Earth* brought eschatology and the pretribulation view into everyday Christian culture—eventually selling over 15 million copies.

Then beginning in 1995, Tim LaHaye's and Jerry B. Jenkins's Left Behind series once again brought the pretribulation view of the rapture (and the literal futurist interpretation method) to the masses on a whole new level—selling almost 80 million copies.

#10 Does Salvation Depend on What Views Are Held?

In the Christian faith, there are core, foundational doctrines (such as the Bible is the Word of God, salvation by grace through faith, the deity of Christ, His substitutionary atonement, bodily resurrection, the Trinity), and important but nonsalvific doctrines that have no bearing on a person's salvation (such as modes of baptism, church government, roles of angels, gifts of the Spirit, and eschatology).

Just as baptism does not save us (1 Peter 3:21), neither does our position on the end times and the return of Christ. Jesus promised the thief on the cross he would be with Him in Paradise on that very day, even though he had no idea there was such a thing as eschatology (Luke 23:43). So, one's view of the end times is not required for salvation and in no way reflects upon a person's standing before God. And this also applies to one's belief concerning the timing of the rapture. Salvation is solely about trusting in Jesus, not in forming a particular belief about the end times.

Even so, it's in the Bible; therefore, it definitely does matter. And one view has to be the correct one, as each of these views mutually excludes the others (i.e., Revelation's judgments cannot simultaneously be both literal *and* figurative). But could the differing views regarding the rapture, tribulation, second coming of Christ, and His kingdom all somehow contain elements of truth to them? And just how important is one's belief in a particular view?

Let's address this with four principles that will help bring all this into perspective.

First, it's okay for Christians to respectfully disagree on some doctrines. It doesn't mean we think less of each other. It's not essential for us to have 100 percent uniformity in every one of our beliefs in order for us to enjoy fellowship and experience unity in Christ.

Second, it is *not* okay for a Christian to remain in ignorance about the end times or to be content with being *unsure* about eschatology. The apostle Paul was very passionate about Christians being informed, confident, and comforted regarding the truths of the last days (1 Thessalonians 4:13-18; 2 Thessalonians 2:1-5). Remaining in ignorance opens us up to false teaching and anxiety, and can even shake our faith. The last book God ever wrote is called Revelation (lit. "unveiling"), which implies knowledge and understanding, not vagueness and lack of information.

Third, interpreting the Bible literally doesn't eliminate all the mystery in prophecy. Not every detail is spelled out for us in Daniel and Revelation, as God hasn't revealed *all* the specifics to us. And that's okay, as it has been His pattern all along.[27] So, there are details no one can know this side of Revelation 6–19.

Fourth, it really does matter *what* you believe, because your view of the end times will dramatically impact your perspective, attitudes, and behavior right now (Titus 2:11-15; 2 Peter 3:14; 1 John 3:1-3).

And that, too, is one of the purposes of Bible prophecy!

CHAPTER 3

THE RAPTURE/APPEARING

#1 Are We Supposed to Watch for Signs?

We are told in 1 Chronicles 12:32 that the leaders of Issachar "understood the times, with knowledge of what Israel should do." The wise men from the east (Matthew 2), the godly old man Simeon (Luke 2), and the old prophetess Anna (Luke 2) all understood the timeframe of the Lord's first arrival, and their amazing stories are recorded for us in Scripture.

We also find that Jesus rebuked the Pharisees and the crowds of people for not knowing the signs of their day. To the scribes and Pharisees He said, "Do you know how to discern the appearance of the sky, but cannot discern the signs of the times?" (Matthew 16:3). To the crowds He said, "You hypocrites! You know how to analyze the appearance of the earth and the sky, but why do you not analyze this present time?" (Luke 12:56).

On one occasion, as Jesus and His disciples were leaving the temple in Jerusalem, He informed them that the beautiful temple and surrounding buildings they were admiring would one day be completely destroyed. Later, His disciples approached Jesus wanting to understand more. In Matthew 24:3 we read, "As [Jesus] was sitting on the Mount of Olives, the disciples came to Him privately, saying, 'Tell us, when will these things happen, and what will be the sign of Your coming, and of the end of the age?'"

Rather than rebuke them or downplay the question, Jesus gave them a full chapter's worth of signs followed by another full chapter of related parables.

This central teaching by Jesus regarding the end-times signs is recorded in three of the four Gospels—in Matthew 24, Mark 13, and Luke 21.

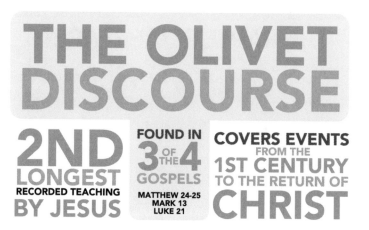

THE OLIVET DISCOURSE

2ND LONGEST RECORDED TEACHING BY JESUS

FOUND IN 3 OF THE 4 GOSPELS
MATTHEW 24-25
MARK 13
LUKE 21

COVERS EVENTS FROM THE 1ST CENTURY TO THE RETURN OF CHRIST

The apostle Paul, whom God used to take Christianity to the Gentiles, realized that the church age was the last age or era before the rapture and the terrible tribulation period. He tells us in Romans 13:11-12, "Do this, knowing the time, that it is already the hour for you to awaken from sleep; for now salvation is nearer to us than when we believed. The night is almost gone, and the day is near. Therefore let us lay aside the deeds of darkness and put on the armor of light." If this was true in Paul's day, it's even truer today since almost 2,000 years have passed. Paul also admonished believers to be watchful and ready.

Finally, the book of Hebrews provides the insight that those living close to Jesus' return will be able to recognize that they are in the season of the Lord's return. Consider the bold statement in the latter part of Hebrews 10:25 where we read, "not forsaking our own assembling together, as is the habit of some, but encouraging one another; and all the more as you see the day drawing near." Clearly, believers at the end of the church age will be able to understand when they are living in the season of the Lord's return.

A careful study of Scripture demonstrates that believers are instructed to watch for the Lord's return and understand their times.

#2 What Did Jesus Teach About Signs?

In the Olivet Discourse, His second longest recorded teaching, Jesus gave a lengthy list of signs that would indicate the end of the church age was approaching. He also described specific events that will take place during the tribulation period, such as Jerusalem being surrounded by an army and the "abomination of desolation" (the Antichrist's defilement of the Jewish temple at the midpoint of the tribulation).

Jesus mentioned many signs heralding His return including false Christs, wars and rumors of wars, persecution, famines, earthquakes, pestilence, and heavenly signs. Jesus also said the gospel would be preached to all nations—then the end of the age would arrive. Jesus said these would be like birth pains, meaning they would increase in frequency and intensity, finding their ultimate or full fulfillment in the future tribulation period.

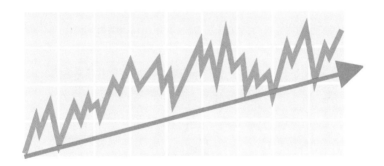

There are two schools of thought from Bible-believing Christians on how the Olivet Discourse should be interpreted. Some assert that Jesus was speaking only to a Jewish audience and that this section has no application for the church. Others argue that, while Jesus was speaking to His Jewish disciples and much of the Olivet Discourse pertains specifically to the tribulation period, it does also have application for the church, just as the Old Testament or Paul's letters to the Thessalonians have application for believers today. Possible support for this second view is the fact that the

Olivet Discourse was also recorded in Mark 13 and Luke 21. Both of these were written for a Gentile audience.

I (Todd) lean toward the second school of thought and believe the Olivet Discourse lists signs that will increase the closer we get to the tribulation period—finding their ultimate maximum intensity in the tribulation period. Interestingly, we see every single one of these signs in our day increasing in frequency and intensity. My good friends who lean toward the other view (that the birth pains are only for the tribulation period) still see these end-time conditions forming in our day in the lead-up to the future seven-year tribulation period after the church is removed and God turns His primary attention to saving Israel and the Jewish people.

The primary puzzle piece needed for any end-time sign to be considered legitimate is the rebirth of Israel (prophesied in Scripture as a key end-time condition). All end-time prophecy centers on the nation of Israel.

A study of Scripture reveals that Israel is depicted as three different plants: the vine, the olive tree, and the fig tree. The vine symbolizes Israel's spiritual privileges. The olive tree symbolizes Israel's religious privileges. But the fig tree always represents Israel's national privileges.

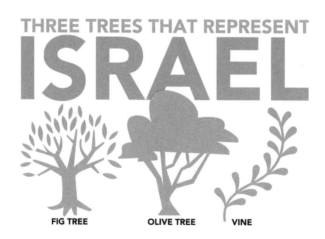

THREE TREES THAT REPRESENT ISRAEL

FIG TREE   OLIVE TREE   VINE

In this incredibly important teaching by Jesus, He also referenced the all-important rebirth of national Israel through the parable of the fig tree. In Matthew 24:32-35 we read:

"Now learn the parable from the fig tree: when its branch has already become tender and puts forth its leaves, you know that summer is near; so, you too, when you see all these things, recognize that He is near, right at the door. Truly I say to you, this generation will not pass away until all these things take place. Heaven and earth will pass away, but My words will not pass away." (See also Mark 13:28-31; Luke 21:29-33.)

In the days leading up to the Olivet Discourse, Jesus entered Jerusalem on a donkey in fulfillment of prophecy—essentially claiming to be king in a very public way. He was then rejected by the Jewish religious leaders. Following this incident with the religious leaders, Jesus cursed a fig tree in front of His disciples and "at once the fig tree withered" (Matthew 21:19). Then we come to Jesus' parable of the fig tree in the context of end-time signs.

Jesus knew Jerusalem would soon be destroyed (Matthew 24:2) and that the Jewish people would be dispersed all over the world for a long period of time before returning to their homeland, which would be reborn in a single day (Isaiah 66:8). The Old Testament has many prophecies about the rebirth of national Israel in the end times. Jesus affirms those prophecies through the parable of the fig tree.

The miraculous rebirth of Israel followed by the many conditions we see developing in our day serve as major signs that we are nearing the time of the rapture followed by the seven-year tribulation period.

#3 What Is the Super-Sign?

Many prophecy experts call Israel the super-sign. All other end-time signs hinge on this one. No other sign of the end could occur until Israel became a nation again. Experts also call it the super-sign because of the sheer magnitude (and statistical impossibility) of this sign coming to pass. Every Old Testament prophet except Jonah predicted that Israel would become a nation again and that Jewish people from around the world would return to their ancient homeland. The reestablishment of the nation of Israel occurred on May 14, 1948, and was an undeniable fulfillment of prophecy.

The three primary texts that provide the clearest details of end-times events (Daniel 9; Jesus' Olivet Discourse in Matthew 24, Mark 13, and Luke 21; and the book of Revelation) require Israel to be a literal nation again, for the Jewish people to be in control of Jerusalem, and for the rebuilding of the temple. The first occurred in 1948 as a result of World Wars I and II. The second occurred in 1967 as a result of the Six-Day War. The third will occur between now and the exact midpoint of the future seven-year tribulation period (Daniel 9:27).

In the Old Testament, God warned Israel of judgment if they continued to stray from Him. As a result of civil war, the country had already been divided into two nations—Israel and Judah—then each nation was attacked. First, in 772 BC the northern nation of Israel was taken captive by Assyria. Then in 586 BC the southern nation of Judah was taken into captivity by the Babylonians. God sent multiple prophets to each nation prior to its judgment, calling the people to turn back to the Lord, but they refused.

After 70 years of captivity, God allowed them to return to their homeland (the first time). As time went on, they drifted from the Lord again and most rejected Christ at His first coming. God then allowed the Romans to destroy Jerusalem in AD 70, and the Jewish people were scattered all over the world—initially regionally, then as the centuries ticked by, globally. They were persecuted and scattered at various times and in various ways in each nation they settled. This was the second, and much more severe, dispersion.

After 1,800 or so years, there were almost no Jewish people living in Israel. During that entire period there was a miraculous drought. Israel became a vast wasteland. By the twentieth century it's estimated there were only 17,000 trees left. There were no trees south of the Sea of Galilee. Nobody wanted this land. But soon after Israel's rebirth weather patterns shifted, technology was developed, and today Israel is a lush and fruitful land that exports crops, cutting-edge technology, and (only recently) gas and oil.

With that backdrop in mind, consider these 2,600-year-old prophecies:

Ezekiel 36:24—"'I will take you from the nations, gather you from all the lands and bring you into your own land.'"

Ezekiel 37:21-22—"'Behold, I will take the sons of Israel from among the nations where they have gone, and I will gather them from every side and bring them into their own land; and I will make them one nation in the land, on the mountains of Israel; and one king will be king for all of them; and they will no longer be two nations and no longer be divided into two kingdoms.'"

Isaiah 11:11—"It will happen on that day that the Lord will again recover *the second time* with His hand [the first being the Babylonian captivity in the sixth century BC] the remnant of his people" (emphasis added).

Jeremiah 16:14-15—"'Therefore behold, days are coming,' declares the Lord, 'when it will no longer be said, "As the Lord lives, who brought up the sons of Israel out of the land of Egypt," but, "As the Lord lives, who brought up the sons of Israel from the land of the north and from all the countries where He had banished them." For I will restore them to their own land which I gave to their fathers.'"

In that last verse, Jeremiah's prophecy reminds us that Israel becoming a nation again was a greater miracle than Moses parting the Red Sea.

This prophecy is repeated four times in the book of Jeremiah just to make sure future generations did not miss its significance. The rebirth of Israel in 1948 was, without question, *the* super-sign that we are nearing the end of the church age.

#4 What Are the Geopolitical Signs?

In addition to the rebirth of the nation of Israel, the Bible also predicted several other specific geopolitical conditions. For example, in Ezekiel 38, we learn of an end-time attack on Israel after her rebirth. It is one of the most detailed prophecies in the Bible and provides several specific details. Among these is a predicted end-time alignment of nations involving Russia, Turkey, and Iran leading a coalition of nations against Israel.

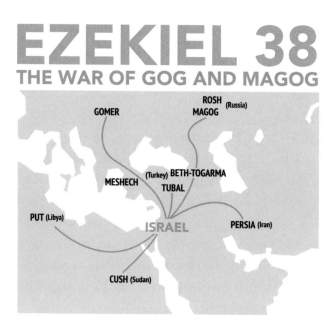

Russia was foretold to be the leader/protector, and the combined forces are prophesied to attack from the northern mountains of Israel (i.e., from

Syria, but Syria will not be a player in the attack) for the purpose of taking something valuable that Israel has. This end-time attack (which God will quickly and supernaturally squash) will be protested by Saudi Arabia (38:13—Sheba and Dedan) along with Tarshish and its villages (lit. "young lions/strong lions"). Many prophecy experts make a strong case that Tarshish is modern-day England (or possibly Spain), making its villages ("young lions") nations that grew out of the British Empire—specifically America. If this is the case, it appears from this prophecy that America will not be in a position to assist Israel militarily.

The stage for this scenario is fully set. The "Arab Spring" and specifically the civil war in Syria (beginning in 2011) became the catalyst for Russia, Iran, and Turkey to fill the political and military void in Syria. This has led to an official partnership between the three nations—along with the other secondary nations listed in the Ezekiel 38 prophecy, such as Libya and Sudan.

It's important to note that America is not found in Bible prophecy as any major superpower in the end times. The current struggles in America (including the effects of COVID-19 and social unrest) could be a foreshadow of America's ultimate weakening. Many prophecy experts believe the rapture of the church will ultimately be what causes America to fully implode. The resulting power vacuum and global economic collapse will set the stage for the rise of the Antichrist.

There are many other geopolitical end-time signs including: the political push for global government by organizations such as the United Nations, the World Economic Forum, the World Health Organization, and other large and small globalist organizations, elite groups, and secret societies; a revived Roman Empire made up of strong and weak nations (European Union) as described in Daniel 2; and the emergence of Far Eastern nations as superpowers (such as China). All of these developments relate to specific end-time prophecies and were predicted 2,000–2,600 years ago.

All of these conditions are setting the stage for the events of the future tribulation period and serve as signs to our generation that we are drawing close to those events.

In the Olivet Discourse, Jesus listed various signs of nature that would increase in frequency and intensity (like birth pains) as we neared the time of the end. In Matthew 24:7-8, we read, "Nation will rise against nation, and kingdom against kingdom, and in various places there will be famines and earthquakes. But all these things are merely the beginning of birth pangs." In Luke 21:11, Jesus adds plagues to the list. Plague can mean pestilence (i.e., a pandemic), but it can also mean any major catastrophe, such as the ten plagues God sent on ancient Egypt through Moses. While these signs will find their apex during the 21 judgments of the future tribulation period, we see them ramping up tremendously in our day.

Pause for a moment and think about the number of unprecedented weather and seismic events that have taken place this century. Whether the plague is wildfires, floods, locust invasions, hurricanes, tornadoes, mass animal deaths, volcanos, or earthquakes—it seems that with each catastrophic event we hear terms such as *record-breaking, unprecedented, once-in-a-lifetime, worst-on-record, of biblical proportions.*

Some of the places that have experienced major earthquakes in recent memory include Haiti, Japan, Indonesia, Chile, and Pakistan. Those quakes caught the world's attention due to their destructive power—tsunamis, staggering loss of life, and horrific video footage. The 2004 Indian Ocean 9.3 earthquake and tsunami killed 230,000–280,000 people. It was the third largest quake ever recorded and had the longest duration ever recorded.

That 9.3 measurement should really get our attention. Many assume that a 1-point increase on the Richter scale (from a 3.0 to a 4.0 for example) is only twice as powerful as the preceding number, but the amount of destructive energy released from the higher number is actually ten times stronger than the previous number. This increases with each point on the scale. So, for example, a 6.0 earthquake is not just six times stronger than a 1.0—it is 100,000 times stronger than a 1.0! The Indian Ocean earthquake was a 9.3. This kind of power is difficult to comprehend and unheard of in the world of seismic study—yet it happened in this century.

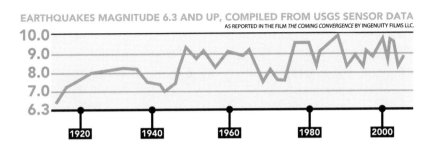

EARTHQUAKES MAGNITUDE 6.3 AND UP, COMPILED FROM USGS SENSOR DATA
AS REPORTED IN THE FILM *THE COMING CONVERGENCE* BY INGENUITY FILMS LLC.

Extreme weather and seismic activity are the natural result of a fallen world that groans in anticipation of redemption (Romans 8:22-23). And the Lord foreknew that as the earth continued to wear out like a garment (Isaiah 51:6), the birth pains of its growing instability would noticeably increase in the lead-up to the appointed end. The nonbelieving world attributes all of these changes to climate change. Whatever the causes, the fact is that Jesus said we would witness a convulsion of nature that would increase in frequency and intensity at the end of the church age—finding its climax in the future tribulation period.

#6 What Are the Spiritual Signs?

Positive Signs

Gospel Preached Worldwide

One of the positive signs we read in the Olivet Discourse is the sign of the gospel preached to the whole world (Matthew 24:14). Jesus' 12 mostly uneducated disciples from an obscure village led a movement that spread the gospel throughout the Roman Empire—reaching portions of the European continent, Asia, and North Africa within a few hundred years.

Fast-forward to the Great Awakening of the 1730s and 1740s, the modern missionary movement of the late 1700s and the mid-1900s, during which God used Billy Graham and a handful of Christian ministries to reach millions with the gospel. Graham preached at 417 crusades in 185 countries on 6 continents and reached more than 210 million people. Fast-forward again to our day, with the Internet now reaching almost every area of the globe. The gospel is literally going to the entire earth.

Revival in the Darkest of Places

While Christianity wanes in the West, for the first time ever, revival is exploding in some of the darkest, most oppressive countries on earth. In Iran, for example, thousands are turning to Christ in response to Internet ministries and Christian programming on satellite television and over radio waves.

Prophecy Unsealed

When God revealed visions about the future to Daniel, he did not understand many of them and was told that his visions were to be sealed—mysteriously incomprehensible and out of reach—until the time of the end. Daniel 12:4,8-9 reads,

> "But you, Daniel, shut up the words, and seal the book until the time of the end; many shall run to and fro, and knowledge shall increase."...Although I heard, I did not understand. Then I said, "My lord, what shall be the end of these things?" And he said, "Go your way, Daniel, *for the words are closed up and sealed till the time of the end*" (NKJV, emphasis added).

What Daniel 12:4 says about knowledge increasing in the time of the end likely has a dual application. Knowledge in general has absolutely exploded, as has the understanding of Bible prophecy. As the world stage continues to be set, prophecies that perplexed experts from a previous generation are now understood with clarity. The closer we get to the tribulation period, the more we seem to understand about end-time prophecy. With each step toward the epicenter of activity, clarity grows and prophecies are unsealed—just as we were told in the book of Daniel.

Negative Signs

There are also negative spiritual signs emerging as predicted. These signs include an increase in false Christs (cults that integrate Jesus or parts of the Bible into their false teachings), apostasy, persecution, the rise of the occult in popular culture, strong delusion and widespread deception, and scoffers and mockers (people making fun of the idea of the Lord's return).

The positive and negative spiritual signs are two sides of the same coin. As we draw near to the Lord's return, our God, who is full of mercy and grace, will extend every opportunity for people to trust in Him before the rapture. Likewise, as Satan sees the same signs we do, he'll do everything in his power to keep people from turning to the only One who can save them.

SPIRITUAL SIGNS

POSITIVE

NEGATIVE

#7 What Are the Cultural Signs?

The following Scripture passage sums it up powerfully when it comes to cultural signs. Read it and think of the current conditions in culture. This 2,000-year-old Pauline prophecy reads like a modern-day description:

> But realize this, that in the last days difficult times will come. For men will be lovers of self, lovers of money, boastful, arrogant, revilers, disobedient to parents, ungrateful, unholy, unloving, irreconcilable, malicious gossips, without self-control, brutal,

haters of good, treacherous, reckless, conceited, lovers of pleasure rather than lovers of God (2 Timothy 3:1-4).

Also, Jesus said that the time period preceding His return would be just like the days of Noah and Lot (Matthew 24:37-39; Luke 17:26-30). Those time periods were characterized by prolific violence and extreme sexual immorality. There has always been violence and sexual immorality, but until recently it has always been a fringe minority. Today, these two characteristics are mainstay features of our world and seemingly getting worse by the day.

Additionally, there has been an exponential growth in drug use and human trafficking in recent decades. In Revelation 9:21, we read about the future reaction of many in the world after several tribulation-period judgments will have occurred. The text informs us that people will still continue to be characterized by murder, stealing, immorality, and "sorceries." The Greek word used is *pharmakeia*—and it means drug use (often combined with occult practice or resulting in occult connections).

One of the things end-time Babylon will be judged for is human trafficking. In Revelation 18, we read about the fall of Babylon in the future tribulation period. John provides a long list of the products that the world will no longer be able to get from Babylon. After listing all the luxury products you would normally think of, the last "product" listed is human lives (v. 13). The black market industries of drugs and human trafficking have emerged (on a global scale) in only the past few decades and continue to grow rapidly.

There are also cultural signs related to morality. As the world falls away from God's truth, it also falls away from God's protective standards of morality. In Romans 1, we read about a progression of immorality resulting in God's abandonment wrath. From the late sixties to today, we've watched the world descend morally, exactly as described in Romans 1.

The cultural signs are all around us. If we take the time to stop and think about how much has changed in our lifetime, or if we do a bit of research about the state of morality prior to the late sixties, we get a clear snapshot of the decline of morality. Immorality has been around since the fall of humankind, but not on the global level it is today where immorality is celebrated and encouraged.

#8 What Are the Technological Signs?

There's an often-overlooked relationship between technology and prophecy. Many predictions in Scripture point to future technology that is necessary for certain foretold events to occur. The prophets of old simply delivered the messages and visions they received from the Lord, often not even understanding much about the prophecies themselves. The fulfillment of many prophecies was not even possible at the time the prophecies were given.

In Daniel 12:4, we read, "But as for you, Daniel, conceal these words and seal up the book until the end of time; many will go back and forth, and knowledge will increase."

One application of this verse is that the end times will be characterized by greatly increased travel and knowledge.

Nuclear weaponry, satellite and Internet broadcasting, massive data centers, DNA manipulation, artificial intelligence, surveillance systems,

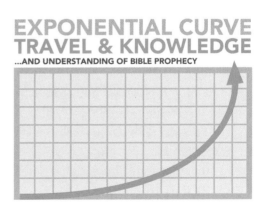

EXPONENTIAL CURVE
TRAVEL & KNOWLEDGE
...AND UNDERSTANDING OF BIBLE PROPHECY

transhumanism, cashless digital currency, and many other current and emerging technologies are described in Bible prophecy or are logically necessary for end-time events to occur. Today, every technology needed to fulfill end-time prophecies exists! All of this has come to pass within the past century or so. In a relatively short period of time, we've gone from riding horses to traveling to the moon; from knowing little about biological design to mapping DNA. Truly we live in the time Daniel prophesied.

One of the specific integrated technology systems needed for a key prophecy to be fulfilled at the midpoint of the future tribulation period is what prophecy experts refer to as "mark of the beast" technology. In Revelation 13:16-17, we read, "And he causes all, the small and the great, and the rich and the poor, and the free men and the slaves, to be given a mark on their right hand or on their forehead, and he provides that no one will be able to buy or to sell, except the one who has the mark, either the name of the beast or the number of his name."

In order for this event to occur as described in God's Word, an unprecedented merge of several technologies must be developed and implemented globally. This system must merge biometrics, a biological (embedded) tracking system, a cashless currency/digital currency, a global database, and super-processing systems run by artificial intelligence. All of these technologies currently exist and are being integrated on an ever-broadening scale.

Some prophecy experts also highlight the possibility that the mark of the beast may also be used to change people in some significant biological way. Revelation tells us that once someone takes the mark of the beast, it is a point of no return and they can no longer be saved (Revelation 14:10-11). We also find that only those who take the mark of the beast will later have painful sores all over their bodies (Revelation 16:2). This could mean that something biological about the mark—such as faulty DNA editing or other emerging technology—will actually cause these sores.

These and several other technological developments are needed for end-time prophecy to be fulfilled. We see all of this technology proliferating in our day. These signs point to an exit ramp coming soon.

#9 What Are the Signs of Convergence?

A convergence occurs when many seemingly unrelated things come together at the same location or point in time. What we're seeing today—literally for the first time in history—is the convergence of all the signs and conditions of the end times.

Like two bookends of the signs categories we've been reviewing, Israel and convergence frame the discussion. On one hand, we have the rebirth of Israel as the first bookend. This super-sign clearly set the end-time clock into motion. On the other end we have the sign of convergence as we see all the signs lining up simultaneously.

A friend of mine used this analogy, which I (Todd) think is a very good one. He says that convergence is like a six-lane highway that slowly but surely funnels into one exit lane.

Another analogy many prophecy experts have used is that of a play about to start. You look around and see that everyone is sitting in their seats and the house is getting full. The curtain on the stage is still closed, but under the curtain you can see feet shuffling around on the stage. You hear lots of commotion behind the curtain and you can sense everything is being set up. All you are waiting for are the lights to dim and the curtain to open—then it's showtime.

The fact that every single end-time sign category is in active play in our day should get our attention. Never before in history has there been such a convergence of events and conditions. These are the days the prophets of old longed to see. While the unbelieving world senses the growing instability, looming wars, impending economic collapse, and the convulsions of nature, they do not know where to turn or how to fix the problems of the day.

Sadly, many in the church have stopped watching and don't see this once-in-history convergence of signs. Some in the church even mock those who highlight the fact that our times identically match the Bible's description of the end of the church age. This too is a sign. In Luke 18:8, Jesus posed a sadly prophetic question when He asked, "When the Son of Man comes, will He find faith on the earth?"

#10 How Close Are We?

All of these sign categories—particularly that of convergence—mean that we are likely very close to the Lord's return. Scripture is clear that "of that day and hour no one knows" (Matthew 24:36), but we can study the many signs and know that His return is drawing near (Matthew 24:33; Luke 21:28; Hebrews 10:25).

There's one other point about convergence that many don't realize. Convergence has a shelf life. When multiple events converge, eventually they unconverge. The stage can be further set, but not indefinitely. The birth pains can increase more, but at some point the baby must be born. In other words, the current convergence of signs and conditions is the most powerful factor that lets us know we are in the season of the Lord's return.

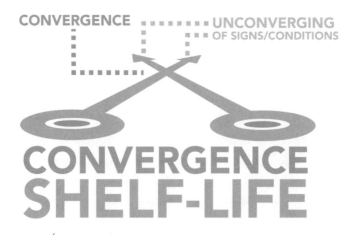

If you'll recall from a few chapters ago, Jesus said in Matthew 24—in the parable of the fig tree—that the generation that sees all of the signs increasing like birth pains after national Israel is reborn would not pass until all the things He talked about (including His return) occur. So the key question is, What is a generation?

Psalm 90:10 reads,

> As for the days of our life, they contain seventy years,
> Or if due to strength, eighty years,
> Yet their pride is but labor and sorrow;
> For soon it is gone and we fly away.

So, it is possible that a generation is 70–80 years. Some even assert that the phrase "and we fly away" could be a veiled reference to the rapture. Others have reasoned that Jesus simply meant that someone from the generation that was alive when Israel became a nation again will still be alive when the Lord returns. While others point to Genesis 6:3 and cite a 120-year time period.

We do not know exactly when the Lord will return, but the fact that all the signs are converging at a time when the world seems to grow more unstable each day—and while we are already past the 70-year mark of Israel's rebirth—leads us to believe time may be shorter than many Christians realize.

If God's Word is truly to be taken literally (we believe it is), and if every single fulfilled prophecy came to pass exactly as foretold and right on time (and they did), then we must conclude that the Lord's return is truly imminent and we are the final generation. Only time will tell and, admittedly, we "see in a mirror dimly" (1 Corinthians 13:12). But Scripture is equally clear that we who are watching will be able to "see the day [the day of the Lord/tribulation period] drawing near" (Hebrews 10:25). Based on everything in this section, it is clear that we are watching its approach.

CHAPTER 4

THE RAPTURE

#1 What Is the Rapture, and Where Do We See It in Scripture?

The rapture is a doctrine that states that Jesus will return to rescue His bride and take her to His Father's house in heaven. With the exception of the posttribulation rapture view, all other views see the rapture as a deliverance from the wrath of God as described in Revelation. The word *rapture* itself is not found in the New Testament, but neither are *missions, Trinity, great commission, incarnation,* or *Christmas*. The word *Bible* isn't even in the Bible. In fact, no English words are found in the original Greek manuscripts of the New Testament. However, like those other words, *rapture* is simply a word used to describe a teaching or doctrine that *is* found in the Bible. It is based on the Greek word *harpazo*, which means "to seize, suddenly snatch away, or take away by force." *Harpazo* is used 14 times in the New Testament, every time referring to something or someone being snatched away or seized.[28] The English word *rapture* comes from a transliteration of Greek (*harpazo*) into

HARPAZO **RAPTURE**

Latin (*rapturo*). In 1 Thessalonians 4:17, *harpazo* is translated into English as "caught up."

So, the real question is: Does the Bible teach the doctrine of the rapture? The answer is yes. We see it (and its timing) in the pattern of God's previous deliverances. Before unleashing His wrath, God always delivers His people. We see it in the case of Enoch prior to the flood—he literally disappeared, being "caught up" to heaven (Genesis 5:24). Both Noah and Lot were removed from God's wrath and protected prior to judgment. Second, we see it in the words of Jesus in John 14:1-3, where He promises to return and take His disciples to His Father's house. We also see the teaching of the rapture in the prophecies of Paul (1 Corinthians 15:51-54; 1 Thessalonians 1:9-10; 4:13-18; 5:9-10; 2 Thessalonians 2:6-7). The portrayal of the church in the book of Revelation also indicates the church will be raptured prior to tribulation-era judgment (Revelation 3:10—"I also will keep you from the hour of testing, that hour which is about to come upon the whole world, to test those who dwell on the earth").

Further, the word *church* is used 20 times in the book of Revelation—19 times in chapters 1–3, and once in chapter 22. But during the time of tribulation upon earth (chapters 6–19), it is mentioned zero times. Instead, the church is portrayed as being in heaven with Christ in chapter 4 (represented by the 24 elders, and returning with Christ in chapter 19:8,14 (clothed in fine linen). All this biblical evidence points to one thing: the rapture is real.

#2 Is the Rapture a Theory or a New Doctrine?

Some harshly criticize the doctrine of the rapture, claiming it doesn't exist, is a relatively recent belief, or is merely an invented doctrine used as a convenient escape clause to prevent suffering in the last days. We've already dealt with the reality of the rapture, so let's turn our attention to these other assertions.

When judging the legitimacy of a Christian belief or teaching, the question is not how long has the doctrine been popular in the church, but rather, is it found in the Bible? However, Jesus' return for His bride can be found in extrabiblical documents dating all the way back to the first century.[29] The early church fathers also attested to a spirit of expectancy concerning the Lord's return for them, up until Augustine in the fourth century. Then, for centuries, this belief was neglected by a sleeping, errant church, much like the teaching of salvation by grace through faith alone, a doctrine that suffered in the church until the reformers came along (early 1500s). However, in terms of authority our greatest appeal is not to church history but to the Scriptures themselves, which give us clarity concerning this issue (John 14:1-3; 1 Corinthians 15:51-55; 1 Thessalonians 4:13-18).

In terms of the rapture doctrine being invented in order to escape suffering and tribulation, nothing could be further from the truth. Christians are nowhere promised exemption from suffering. Both Jesus and Paul made that abundantly clear (John 15:18-25; 16:20-22; 2 Timothy 2:3; 3:10-13). But there is a vast difference between going through tribulation and going through *the* tribulation. God's deliverance of Enoch, Noah, and Lot was not a convenient escape clause but the demonstration of His heart and His commitment to His children. From this, we can be confident that the rapture is neither a novel theory nor an escape clause from last-days sufferings.

> Jesus' return for His bride can be found in extrabiblical documents dating all the way back to the first century.

#3 What Is the Doctrine of Imminence?

There is a difference between prophecies whose fulfillment dates are unknown and those that are specifically portrayed as imminent. For example, prophecies concerning the regathering of Israel as a nation were unknown in their fulfillment, but it was not generally considered that it could happen at any moment in history.[30] On the other hand, the rapture *could* occur at any time. This is the essence of *imminence*, meaning there is nothing that precedes this event. There are no fulfilled prophecies needed or required in order for the rapture to occur. It is a sign-less event. Therefore, we are not looking for signs of the rapture but for Christ Himself. And where is the biblical evidence for this doctrine of imminence?

> **There are no prophecies that need to be fulfilled in order for the rapture to occur. It is a sign-less event.**

In John 14:1-3, Jesus told His disciples He was leaving them to go prepare a place for them in His Father's house. He promised them He would one day return and take them there. To those in the upper room that night, this was clearly a metaphorical reference to the Jewish wedding custom of the day. Once a man was betrothed to his wife, he returned to his father's house for a period of time, during which he would construct a room or addition onto the house for the newly married couple to live in. At an appointed time set by the father, the groom-to-be appeared unannounced, snatching up his bride and taking her away to his father's house where the marriage would be consummated. Jesus is clearly here not speaking about His second coming at the end of the tribulation, because at that time the church returns *down* to the earth *with* Christ (Revelation 19:7-8,13-14). Rather, in John's passage, the bride is headed in the opposite direction as He takes her *up* to heaven (the Father's house).

For this reason (imminence), the bride was always to be ready for her beloved to appear. And this is exactly what we see in the rest of the New Testament, as this perpetual anticipation for the imminent rapture return of Jesus was regularly on the minds of the early church. This is precisely why we are told to "look for" and to "hope for" the appearing of Christ at the rapture, which could occur at any time.

- Romans 13:11,12—"knowing the *time*, that it is *already* the hour…The night is almost gone, and the day is *near*"[31]

- 1 Corinthians 1:7—"as you *eagerly await* the revelation of our Lord Jesus Christ"

- 1 Corinthians 16:22—"*Maranatha*" (early church greeting, from an Aramaic expression meaning "our Lord, come")

- Philippians 3:20—"for our citizenship is in heaven, from which also we *eagerly wait* for a Savior"

- Philippians 4:5—"the Lord is *near*"

- 1 Thessalonians 1:10—"to *wait* for His Son from heaven"

- Titus 2:13—"*looking for the blessed hope* and the *appearing* of the glory of our great God and Savior, Christ Jesus"

- James 5:8—"be patient; strengthen your hearts, for the coming of the Lord is *near*"

Only a pretribulation rapture truly can be imminent. All other rapture views (midtrib, posttrib, prewrath) can be predicted by looking at the calendar. But because the rapture could happen at any moment, we are looking not for signs but for a Savior.

#4 What Are the Details of the Rapture?

Bible prophecy can sometimes be very specific. And such is the case in 1 Thessalonians 4:13-18. Here, Paul breaks down the chronology of the rapture frame by frame, allowing us to see it in "super slow mo." Here is the order of events:

1. Jesus Himself descends from heaven (remember, He hasn't been here for 2,000 years).

2. He issues a commanding shout (v. 16).[32] This loud command will be heard by every believer alive all over the world.

3. It is immediately followed by another voice, this time an archangel (perhaps Michael), who is most likely announcing the arrival of the bridegroom.

4. The trumpet of God is then sounded, summoning Christ's bride together.

5. Instantly, a grand-scale miracle is performed by Jesus as the decomposed bodies of those believers throughout the church age who have died are supernaturally re-formed and transformed into new resurrection bodies and reunited with their spirits coming from heaven.

6. Christians who are alive at this time will be "caught up" (*harpazo* = raptured) together with those resurrected bodies. At this time those living believers receive their own resurrected bodies (1 Corinthians 15:51-54).

7. Both groups of believers meet the Lord in the air (v. 17). This officially begins heaven for those believers as from this point on "we will always be with the Lord."

These seven supernatural happenings make up this event we know as the rapture. It will be the most dramatic and supernatural occurrence since the ascension of Christ in Acts 1. It also facilitates a joyful reunion with those who have gone on before us. It is at the rapture that our faith becomes sight (1 Corinthians 13:12). The one thing every Christian has longed for his or her entire life will finally be real. We will at last be with Jesus and be complete. Can you think of anything more wonderful or glorious than this? Is it any wonder that Paul concludes by encouraging us to "comfort one another with these words" (v. 18)?

1 TRUMPET. 2 VOICES. 2 TRANSFORMATIONS. 1 GRAND REUNION.

#5 Can Anyone Know When the Rapture Will Occur?

In 1988, Edgar C. Whisenant published a book titled *88 Reasons Why the Rapture Will Be in 1988*. When his prediction proved to be false, he published another book explaining why the rapture will happen in 1989! Other so-called prophetic voices began jumping on the bandwagon, making predictions about Christ's return in 1994, 2011, and most recently 2017, due to a rare planetary alignment. I (Jeff) was interviewed in a DirecTV documentary titled *The Sign* in which some claimed this planetary configuration was a fulfillment of Revelation 12 and that it would usher in the return of Jesus for the church. I was clear in pointing out that not only does Revelation 12 have nothing to do with the rapture, but also that nowhere in Scripture does it indicate that any man can know when it will happen, until of course it actually does.

A verse that is often cited is Matthew 24:36, where Jesus says, "But about that day and hour no one knows, not even the angels of heaven, nor the Son, but the Father alone." However, in this passage Christ is talking about His second coming and not the rapture. During Jesus' earthly ministry, He voluntarily chose to limit some of His divine attributes, instead depending solely on the Father for His revelation/information. Once resurrected and ascended to heaven, He of course resumed all of His sovereignty and omniscience.

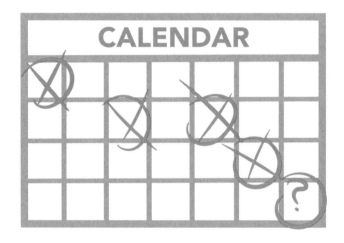

No one can predict the exact timing of the rapture because there are no prophetic signs preceding this event, and Christians are never told when it will happen. However, it is possible to recognize the season and signs that indicate Revelation's prophecies may not be far off (see chapter 1). Hebrews 10:25 speaks of the necessity of gathering together as the church in the last days, and "encouraging one another; and all the more, as you *see the day* drawing near." Some scholars debate whether "the day" refers to the rapture, the second coming, or the destruction of Jerusalem in AD 70. The author appears to be referring to the rapture in 9:28—"Christ...will appear a second time for salvation without reference to sin, to those who eagerly await Him." However, later in chapter 10 he references the second coming (v. 37). Hebrews 10:25 is most likely pointing toward the day of

Christ's second coming, as we are able to see the day drawing near (signs of His return). This is significant, as other Bible prophecy experts have pointed out, because if we can see signs of the future tribulation right now, how close might the rapture be? So, while it is futile and unbiblical to make predictions about the exact timing of the rapture, it is certainly reasonable to conclude that, unlike any other time in church history, the long shadows of Revelation's prophecies are being cast onto our present age. Therefore, the rapture may be sooner than we think.

#6 What Will Our New Bodies Be Like?

The rapture is a doctrine of deliverance from God's wrath, which is poured out during the tribulation (1 Thessalonians 1:10; 5:9; Revelation 3:10). But it also proves to be a deliverance from the temptations of the sin nature and from sin itself, as we are transformed at this time into our glorified state (Romans 8:30; Colossians 3:4; Revelation 22:3). At the rapture, Adam's curse in us will be reversed and "we will be like Him," completely clothed in His righteousness, inside and out (1 Corinthians 15:56-57; 1 John 3:2; Revelation 19:7-8). For those alive at the time of the rapture, their mortal bodies will be supernaturally transformed into glorified ones, and as Paul puts it, "We will all be changed" (1 Corinthians 15:51-55).

Scripture tells us several exciting things about these new bodies:

1. They are not susceptible to aging, sin, disease, or death (Isaiah 53:5; Matthew 8:17; 1 Corinthians 15:53-55; Revelation 21:4).

2. They will be like Jesus' glorified body. Philippians 3:20-21 states: "For our citizenship is in heaven, from which we also eagerly wait for a Savior, the Lord Jesus Christ, who will transform the body of our lowly condition into conformity with His glorious body, by the exertion of the power that He

has even to subject all things to Himself." And what is Jesus' resurrected, glorified body like?

3. They will be physical but unlike the ones we inherited from the first Adam (1 Corinthians 15:42-50; Luke 24:39).

4. Presumably, we will be able to consume food in the millennial kingdom and in the new Jerusalem (Luke 22:16; 24:42-43; Acts 10:40-41; Revelation 19:9; 22:1-2,14,17).

5. These bodies will be free from the physical limitations we once experienced on earth. God designed our current bodies for our earthly atmosphere. But at the rapture, our transformed bodies will be formatted for heaven's environment. In other words, we will be able to dwell in God's presence and withstand His glory, majesty, and holiness.

Paul described God as "He who is the blessed and only Sovereign, the King of kings and Lord of lords; who alone possesses immortality and dwells in unapproachable light, whom no one has seen or can see" (1 Timothy 6:15-16). When the apostle John was exposed to the glorified Christ in his Revelation vision, it traumatized his body and central nervous system to the point where he fell down as a dead man (Revelation 1:12-18). But in our new glorified bodies made possible by the rapture, we will have access to God in His very presence (Revelation 21:3-4; 22:3-5).

Scripture doesn't tell us all of the abilities our new bodies will possess. But we can only imagine that they will be more wonderful and amazing than any human writer could conceive. The concepts of time, space, and travel will be redefined in ways we currently do not know.

#7 What Will We Do in Heaven Between the Rapture and the Second Coming?

One of the most frequent questions I (Jeff) get is "What will we do in heaven?" Typically, when people ask this question, they are referring to our eternal state in heaven. I will address this topic more fully in chapter 10. But what about the time we spend in heaven following the rapture and *before* we return with Jesus at the second coming?

Fortunately, Scripture does give us a sneak peek into this. I, along with most Bible scholars, interpret the 24 elders of Revelation 4 to be representative of the church, the bride of Christ. Among the reasons for this view is that national Israel has not yet been redeemed, and the tribulation saints are not yet saved (Revelation 7:9-10). These 24 elders are also pictured as clothed in white garments and wearing golden crowns on their heads (1 Corinthians 9:24-25; 1 Thessalonians 2:19; 2 Timothy 4:7-8; 1 Peter 5:4; James 1:12; Revelation 2:10). This also describes the church age saints (Revelation 4:1-11; 19:7-8).

Also, that the elders have already received their crowns indicates the bride of Christ will face the bema, or the judgment seat of Christ, immediately following the rapture, not when an individual believer dies (Romans 14:10-12; 1 Corinthians 3:10-15; 4:5; 2 Corinthians 5:10). The bride is already wearing fine linen, representing the reward for her righteous acts done while on earth (Revelation 19:7-8). Among the things we will do during this time is worship, honor, and praise the One who sits on the throne (Revelation 4:9-10). Our understanding of God will also be perfected, enabling us to more fully ascribe to Him the honor He justly deserves (4:11). We will join all the redeemed from the church age in this massive worship gathering (Revelation 5:11-14; 7:11-12).

Scripture indicates that we will also witness the events of the tribulation from heaven (Revelation 11:15-18). You may wonder how we could be happy in heaven knowing that God's wrath is being poured out on the earth during this seven-year period. But keep in mind, at this point we have been completely changed—body, mind, and soul. Now that we're complete, we see and understand everything from God's perspective. Because of this, we can embrace divine justice and retribution upon the wicked who dwell upon the earth, and even give God praise because of it (11:17). We will witness the praise of the 144,000, hearing music in the song that has never been sung before (Revelation 14:1-3). We will have a front-row seat to the most dramatic season in all of human history.

#8 What Will Our New Living Spaces Be Like?

In John 14:2-3, Jesus told His disciples that His Father's house contained many "rooms," promising that He would go there and prepare a place for them. Of course, we know that Christ always honors and fulfills His promises. But what are these rooms like? And are we talking about literal physical spaces or something else? Prior to beginning His public ministry, Jesus most likely worked in Joseph's carpenter shop (Matthew 13:55). So will He put some of His carpentry skills to use in heaven? Or does that miss the point altogether?

First, let's consider the context of these verses. Jesus spoke these words during His last meal with the disciples prior to being arrested and crucified. He knew His closest friends were about to face a devastating punch in the gut as their Lord would be taken from them, unjustly tried, brutally beaten beyond recognition, and violently nailed to a rough wooden cross. Because of this, Jesus gave them these words of hope that would save them from despair after He eventually ascended to heaven (Acts 1:6-11). In fact, this promised return for us is called the "blessed hope" (Titus 2:13). So, the main reason Jesus told His disciples these things was to let them know that this was not the end, and that even while they were separated, He would be thinking of them and preparing for the day when they would join Him in heaven.

But just what are these places He would prepare? First, Jesus used a word (translated "mansions," "rooms," or "dwelling places") that literally means an "abode" or a "place to abide."

As we have already seen, the Jewish custom of the day was that after the engagement, the groom-to-be would return to his father's house and build on an extra room or addition in which the newly married couple would live. Jesus used this custom to illustrate a spiritual reality. He would go back to heaven, and by virtue of His sacrificial death for us, create a place for us to dwell with Him and His Father in heaven. Some see these many rooms in the Father's house referring to the new Jerusalem, which descends to the earth following the millennial kingdom (Revelation 21:1-3,9-27).

The main idea is that we, as the bride of Christ, are all together with our beloved. We will have access to God and His throne, and that reality will far exceed the joy of living in a 50-room mansion. Earthly customs and illustrations cannot fully depict the glory, splendor, and enjoyment of heaven's realities. And the attraction in that day will not be so much *where* we live, but *with Whom* we abide.

#9 Why Hasn't the Rapture Happened Yet?

One of the biggest criticisms of a belief in the rapture is that Christians have been talking about Jesus' return for some 2,000 years. And yet, He hasn't come back, which causes some to think we are superstitious fanatics trusting in a religious fairy tale. However, the apostle Peter, writing under the inspiration of the Holy Spirit, prophesied that in the last days this very belief would indeed be mocked:

> Know this first of all, that in the last days mockers will come with their mocking, following after their own lusts, and saying, "Where is the promise of His coming? For ever since the fathers fell asleep, all things continue just as they were from the beginning of creation" (2 Peter 3:3-4).

So why is it taking Jesus so long to come back for us? What is His delay? We believe He is waiting for two conditions to be met.

The prophetic stage to be set. God is orchestrating both prophecy and history to strategically collide at a prespecified point in time. We know that following the rapture, Antichrist will sign a peace treaty with Israel, officially beginning the seven-year tribulation (Daniel 9:27). This will then set in motion the events and judgments of Revelation 6–19. Some of those prophesied realities (mark of the beast, revived Roman Empire, rebuilt Jewish temple, globalist mindset) will not occur overnight, but rather come together in their initial stages prior to the rapture. In fact, that is exactly what we see happening right now in our world. So in the providence of God, it seems as though He is putting some, though not all, of those puzzle pieces into place prior to the rapture.

CLOCK
OF THE GENTILES

ALMOST MIDNIGHT

The lost to be saved. In Luke 21:24, Jesus refers to "the times of the Gentiles," which many believe covers the period of time between Israel's Babylonian captivity (586 BC) and when she is spiritually restored in the millennial kingdom (Revelation 20:1-6). However, in Romans 11:25, Paul tells us the beginnings of this spiritual restoration will not occur until the "fullness of the Gentiles has come in." In context, he is likely referring to the number of Gentiles that will be redeemed during the church age prior to the rapture. Once the last Gentile has called upon the name of the Lord to be saved (Romans 10:13), Christ will return for His bride. It is in light of this promised return, and unbelievers' mocking of it, that God highlights His patience toward sinners, giving them a wide opportunity to be saved (2 Peter 3:9).

PROPHETIC GAUGES

LAST GENTILE   **PATIENCE METER**

Once these two conditions are met, God will initiate the rapture, which will create a global crisis out of which the Antichrist will arise and the tribulation will begin.

#10 How Will Those Who Are Left Behind Explain the Rapture?

There is no way to fully know how those who are left behind will explain the worldwide disappearance of hundreds of millions. In the Internet generation, where billions can make their voices heard, there will no doubt be an untold number of opinions, theories, conspiracies, and claimed psychic explanations. It is highly likely that these explanations will come also from various cultural entities as well, including scientists, philosophers, religious leaders, and government officials. Even climate change experts may weigh in on the debate. But what will they say? Again, it's impossible to know for sure, but it is reasonable to assume that some will claim Christians have been abducted by some alien intelligence. Others may postulate that God Himself (or whatever supreme being exists) has taken those bigoted, narrow-minded Christians out of the way so that the world can now live in peace and love. Many will also no doubt realize it was the prophesied rapture. And due to their hardened hearts prophesied in the coming delusion, they may not even care (2 Thessalonians 2:10-12).

At the same time, imagine the level of panic and chaos created by this global event. Parents suddenly left without children and children without parents. Spouses separated, coworkers, bosses, and friends unexpectedly vanish. The stock market will plummet, spiraling the global economy to an all-time low. There will be suicide attempts in every part of the world, as people find themselves emotionally unable to deal with the loss of loved ones. Depression, despair, violence, and looting will explode on an unprecedented scale. And on the whole, as we trace through the book of Revelation, we find that mankind does not get any better after the rapture, but rather much worse, even to the point of vehemently refusing to repent. They will dive even deeper into demon worship, murders, rampant drug abuse, widespread immorality, and thefts (Revelation 9:20-21). Further, they even begin blaspheming God because of the judgments He is sending upon them (Romans 1:18-32; 2 Timothy 3:1-5; Revelation 6:15-17; 16:8-11).

As briefly noted earlier, the Bible tells us that during this time there will also be a great deception presented by the Antichrist along with a deluding influence sent by God Himself (2 Thessalonians 2:10-12). So whatever explanations are proposed, we can be pretty certain the vast majority of them will flow from hearts blackened by sin, deceived by Satan, and suffering under a judgment of delusion sent from God.

It is also feasible to conclude from Scripture that many will come to Christ during this time, having previously been warned of the rapture (Revelation 7:9-17). Perhaps they will find their way to Christ through Bibles and books, videos and podcasts left behind. Blogs, social media posts, and memories of conversations they had with believers will come flooding into their minds, perhaps motivating them to fall on their knees and cry out for salvation. And through these new converts the true explanation of the rapture will be shared with others, along with the message of hope and salvation found in Jesus Christ in the midst of this awful time of judgment.

CHAPTER 5

THE JEWISH PEOPLE/ISRAEL

#1 Has the Church Replaced Israel in God's Plans for the Future?

The church has not replaced Israel and the Jews are still God's chosen people. This is a very important aspect of end-time Bible prophecy. Some of God's promises to Israel were conditional, based on their obedience—with prophesied consequences if they disobeyed (Deuteronomy 28). They did disobey and those prophesied consequences came to pass. In addition to the conditional promises, God also gave many specific and unconditional promises to (and prophecies about) Israel.

In Genesis 15:12-19, God made a one-way, unconditional covenant with Abraham regarding several things, including the promise of the land of Israel to Abraham's descendants. Israel has never

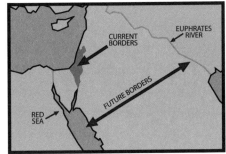

ISRAEL'S BORDERS
IN THE FUTURE MILLENNIAL KINGDOM

occupied the full breadth of the land specified by God—essentially from the Red Sea to the Euphrates River (Exodus 23:31)—in this ancient unconditional covenant.

There are also many very specific prophecies in Psalms, Isaiah, Jeremiah, Ezekiel, Daniel, Hosea, Micah, Matthew, Luke, and Revelation about a future golden age when the Messiah will rule the entire world from Jerusalem, when the animal kingdom will have no carnivores, and the topography of Jerusalem will be completely changed.

These kingdom prophecies obviously have not been fulfilled yet, and will be fulfilled in the future millennial kingdom following the seven-year tribulation period. These clear and specific prophetic details (which make up a sizeable portion of Scripture) would have to be allegorized, ignored, or otherwise explained away if God does not have future plans for Israel.

If there were any doubt about the permanence of God's program for the Jewish people, in Genesis 17:7, God said in crystal-clear terms, "I will establish My covenant between Me and you and your descendants after you throughout their generations as an everlasting covenant, to be God to you and to your descendants after you." In response to people saying God would reject His chosen people, Jeremiah 33:25 records God's clear declaration, "I would no more reject my people than I would change my laws that govern night and day, earth and sky" (NLT).

In the New Testament, Paul echoes this fact in Romans 11:1-2 where he asks (and answers) the rhetorical question, "I say then, God has not rejected His people, has He? Far from it! For I too am an Israelite, a descendant of Abraham, of the tribe of Benjamin. God has not rejected His people whom He foreknew."

Paul concludes this section of Romans (about the difference between God's program for Israel and the church) clearly pointing to a future day at the end of the church age when Israel will corporately turn to the true Messiah for salvation. In Romans 11:25-26, he says, "For I do not want you, brothers and sisters, to be uninformed of this mystery—so that you will not be wise in your own estimation—that a partial hardening has happened to Israel *until the fullness of the Gentiles has come in; and so all Israel will be saved*" (emphasis added). Paul was referring to the future moment Jesus prophesied about when He said, "For I say to you, from now on you will not see Me until you say, 'Blessed is the One who comes in the name of the LORD!'" (Matthew 23:39).

Individually, all people must accept Christ as their Savior in order to be saved (Acts 4:12; Romans 3:23-31; 10:1-4). Corporately, God has very distinct purposes for the church and for Israel. If God breaks His unconditional promises to Israel, how can we trust His unconditional promises to the church?

#2 What Are the Main Views About the Relationship Between Israel and the Church?

There are primarily three approaches to understanding the relationship between the church and Israel: replacement theology, covenant theology, and dispensationalism.

Replacement theology (also known as supersessionism) teaches that the church has replaced Israel and that all promises to Israel are now conferred onto the church. This view does not hold that the Jews are still God's chosen people or that God has any specific future plans for Israel. While not intrinsically antisemitic, this view has often led to antisemitism. Even the great reformer Martin Luther wrote a book based on replacement theology called *On the Jews and Their Lies,* which urged their persecution. Hitler later leveraged Luther's book to support his murderous antisemitic aspirations.

Covenant theology (favored by Reformed/Calvinistic theologians) teaches that the church is an expansion, offshoot, or continuation of Israel. The basis of covenant theology (stated in simplified terms) is that it sees two overarching covenants in Scripture—the covenant of works and the covenant of grace. It sees the church as in essence having been in existence since God first established a covenant of grace with Adam. It sees the Jewish people as being a starting point, so to speak, that would grow to include elect believers from all nations. Covenant theology necessarily allegorizes Scripture and ignores specific unconditional prophecies about Israel and the Jewish people that have never been fulfilled. It views end-time prophecy as allegory and does not view the modern rebirth of Israel as a fulfillment of prophecy.

The third approach, which we believe is the correct one, is that the Bible should be consistently interpreted literally from Genesis to Revelation. The conclusions from this approach clearly demonstrate that God has two distinct programs—one for Israel and one for the church—and that He has worked progressively in different time periods of biblical history. This is known as *dispensationalism* or *premillennialism*. This view acknowledges the clear fact that the church is no longer under the law of the Mosaic covenant and that salvation comes through faith in Jesus Christ alone. But it also acknowledges the unconditional promises related to the Abrahamic covenant, and awaits the literal fulfillment of future prophecies related to Israel and the Jewish people. It views the modern rebirth of Israel as literal fulfilled prophecy.

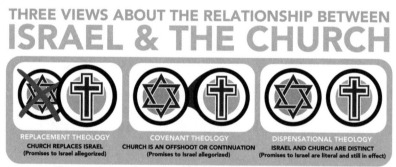

THREE VIEWS ABOUT THE RELATIONSHIP BETWEEN
ISRAEL & THE CHURCH

REPLACEMENT THEOLOGY	COVENANT THEOLOGY	DISPENSATIONAL THEOLOGY
CHURCH REPLACES ISRAEL (Promises to Israel allegorized)	CHURCH IS AN OFFSHOOT OR CONTINUATION (Promises to Israel allegorized)	ISRAEL AND CHURCH ARE DISTINCT (Promises to Israel are literal and still in effect)

All 3 views believe in a personal decision to follow Christ for salvation.

This view squares with Scripture using a consistent hermeneutic from Genesis to Revelation. It teaches that individual salvation is by grace through faith, but that God still has distinct purposes (and yet-unfulfilled future prophecies) for both Israel and the church. Both groups will merge beautifully in the future millennial kingdom and ultimately in the future eternal state.

Prophetically speaking, there are large sections of Scripture that very clearly describe Israel reemerging as a nation and then experiencing a glorious kingdom age. Isaiah and Jeremiah both include a vast amount of prophetic detail about this future time period. Furthermore, the book of Revelation (supported by Daniel 9) clearly demonstrates that God's focus will shift back to His program for Israel during the future seven-year tribulation period. This period is also known as the seventieth week of Daniel (Daniel 9:27), and the time of Jacob's (not the church's) trouble (Jeremiah 30:7).

Of the 404 verses in the book of Revelation, there are over 800 direct allusions to the Old Testament. We find 144,000 Jewish evangelists, two Jewish witnesses, and the centering of world events on Israel, Jerusalem, and the temple mount. Revelation 12 clearly centers the main purpose of the future tribulation period on God's plan for His chosen people. Revelation 20:1-7 clearly gives us the timeframe in which all of the Old Testament kingdom promises will be fulfilled.

We also see the combined symbolism in the future new heavens, new earth, and new Jerusalem. We'll explore the new heavens and new earth for eternity, but our dwelling places will be in the eternal capital—the new Jerusalem. In John's description of the new Jerusalem in Revelation 21:10-14 we discover that it will have 12 gates named after the 12 tribes of Israel and it will have 12 foundations named after the 12 apostles. We will be reminded throughout all eternity of God's distinct—yet perfectly unified—programs for Israel and the church.

#3 Are the Jewish People Key to End-Time Prophecy?

Yes. Many Old Testament prophecies detail the dispersion, mistreatment, and return of the Jewish people to their homeland in the end-times.

The last four verses of Daniel 9 provide an overview of God's prophetic plans for the Jewish people from Daniel's time until the end. A careful study of that text makes it abundantly clear that the Jewish people play a key role in end-time events.

THE 70 WEEKS OF DANIEL
CHAPTER NINE

The final book of the Bible, Revelation, highlights the end of the church age and how God's focus shifts back to Israel. As highlighted in the previous section, the 404 verses of Revelation contain over 800 direct references to the Old Testament and feature several important Jewish figures. There are two Jewish witnesses, 144,000 Jewish evangelists (12,000 from each tribe), and a clear focus on Israel, Jerusalem, and an end-time Jewish temple.

During the tribulation period, the church will be with Jesus in heaven (Revelation 4:1-5,9-11) while God judges the evil world system and focuses on turning the hearts of the Jewish people to the true Messiah (Revelation 7:1-8; 11:3-12; 12:1-6; 14:1-4). Jesus specifically said in Matthew 23:37, "Jerusalem, Jerusalem, who kills the prophets and stones those who have been sent to her! How often I wanted to gather your children together, the way a hen gathers her chicks under her wings, and you were unwilling." Then He says in verse 39, "You will not see Me until you say, 'Blessed is the One who comes in the name of the Lord!'" Basically, He was saying, "Judgment is coming, and you will be scattered over the earth and blinded to the truth of who I am until a specific point where you will realize I was the Messiah you were expecting."

Paul provides more insight in Romans 9–11. In 11:25, he points out that "a partial hardening has happened to Israel until the fullness of the Gentiles has come in." To make sure everyone knows God's plan for Israel didn't end there, he then makes the clear statement in the next verse that "all Israel will be saved." At the end of the tribulation period when the dragon (Satan indwelling the Antichrist) is pursuing and persecuting the Jews (see Revelation 12), they will be protected and will corporately turn to the Lord as their true Messiah. The salvation of Israel is the exclamation point at the end of the biblical narrative. Christ will return to earth to set up the kingdom when Israel's blindness is gone and they finally realize Jesus was their true Messiah.

As mentioned above, after the tribulation, the church and Israel will blend in a beautiful way. In eternity there will be an eternal city known as the new Jerusalem. It will feature 12 gates having the names of the 12 tribes of Israel (Revelation 21:12), and 12 foundations featuring the names of the 12 apostles (Revelation 21:14). Israel (all Jewish people who accepted Christ) and the church (all non-Jewish people who accepted Christ) will merge seamlessly and enjoy God's presence together for all of eternity.

It is important to remember that every book of the Bible was written by a Jewish person, our Savior Jesus Christ is (not was) Jewish, and every single person who was part of the birth of the church on Pentecost was Jewish. The church age is a sovereignly planned parenthesis in God's plan for His chosen people.

#4 Is the Nation of Israel Key to End-Time Prophecy?

Yes, absolutely. It is the most critical component. All of the key prophetic end-time texts, including Ezekiel 38, Daniel 9, Matthew 24, Mark 13, Luke 21, and several chapters in Revelation, all necessarily require Israel to exist as a nation. As mentioned in chapter 3 regarding end-time signs, prophecy experts refer to Israel's rebirth as the *super-sign*. First, because all other end-time events hinge on this one sign being in place. Second, experts call it the super-sign because of the sheer magnitude and impossibility of it taking place by chance or historical coincidence. Every Old Testament prophet except Jonah prophesied that Israel would be reborn in the end times.

Since the fulfillment of all end-time prophecies hinges on the nation of Israel being in existence, modern Israel is referred to by many prophecy teachers as end-time prophecy's timepiece. It has even been stated that Israel is the clock, Jerusalem is the hour hand, and the temple mount in Old Jerusalem is the minute hand. Israel's rebirth signals the prophetic fact that we are living near the time of the end.

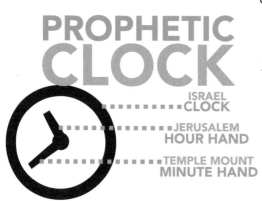

Satan has done a great job blinding many believers to the prophetic significance of the rebirth of Israel in 1948. Many people in the church have never been taught about this mind-blowing fulfillment of Bible prophecy. The fact that it was prophesied many times in both the Old and New Testaments should help us see how profound this modern-day fulfillment is. It is the key indicator that the church age is winding down. The rebirth of Israel in 1948 was not a random historical event in geopolitics. It was a specific fulfillment of prophecy foretold with incredible accuracy—2,600 years in the making!

#5 Is Jerusalem Key to End-Time Prophecy?

Yes. Among other reasons (some detailed below), Daniel (9:27) and Jesus (Matthew 24:15-16; Mark 13:14) both mention the abomination of desolation—a midtribulation event when the Antichrist will defile the yet-to-be rebuilt Jewish temple. Additionally, Jesus informed His disciples that in the end times, Jerusalem would be surrounded at this point. In Revelation 12, John provides more information. The Antichrist will break his covenant with the Jewish people at the exact midpoint of the future tribulation period, then he will turn on them in hot pursuit—attempting to destroy every Jewish person on earth. Thankfully, God will protect a remnant who will turn to the Lord at the end of the tribulation.

JERUSALEM
THE EPICENTER OF BIBLE PROPHECY

We also discover other direct prophecies about Jerusalem in the end times. The prophecy below was written after the Jewish people had returned from Babylonian captivity. Zechariah was written roughly 500 years before Christ and 570 years before the Romans would attack Jerusalem and destroy the temple. In other words, this prophecy didn't make sense to the generation it was written to because the Jewish people were already back in Jerusalem, having returned from their captivity in Babylon.

> "The LORD of armies says this: 'Old men and old women will again sit in the public squares of Jerusalem, each person with his staff in his hand because of age. And the public squares of the city will be filled with boys and girls playing in its squares.' The LORD of armies says this: 'If it is too difficult in the sight of the remnant of this people in those days, will it also be too difficult

in My sight?' declares the LORD of armies. The LORD of armies says this: 'Behold, I am going to save My people from the land of the east and from the land of the west; and I will bring them back and they will live in the midst of Jerusalem; and they shall be My people, and I will be their God in truth and righteousness'" (Zechariah 8:4-8).

Later in the book, Zechariah also foretells more details about Jerusalem in the future tribulation period, also known as the Day of the Lord (note the term "that day" below). We read this in chapter 12.

"Behold, I am going to make Jerusalem a cup that causes staggering to all the peoples around; and when the siege is against Jerusalem, it will also be against Judah. It will come about on that day that I will make Jerusalem a heavy stone for all the peoples; all who lift it will injure themselves severely. And all the nations of the earth will be gathered against it" (Zechariah 12:2-3).

This next verse is very compelling because Luke records Jesus' famous end-time teaching (the Olivet Discourse), and here Jesus notes a key detail about Jerusalem that has been partially fulfilled in our day: "They will fall by the edge of the sword, and will be led captive into all the nations; and Jerusalem will be trampled underfoot by the Gentiles until the times of the Gentiles are fulfilled" (Luke 21:24).

In this single verse, Jesus predicted the Jewish people would be attacked, kicked out of their land, dispersed all over the world, and that Jerusalem would be under non-Jewish control. All of this happened exactly as foretold. But notice Jesus indicated there would be an end to the non-Jewish control of Jerusalem.

On June 7, 1967, the end of the Six-Day War saw Jerusalem conquered and reoccupied by Israel. For the first time in 1,897 years, the Jewish people were in sovereign control of their ancient capital. This was a major modern-day fulfillment of Bible prophecy—setting the stage for the return of Christ.

#6 What Is the Abrahamic Covenant?

The Abrahamic covenant is a specific, literal, and unconditional covenant between God, Abraham, and—by extension—Abraham's descendants, the Jewish people. We read about the covenant in Genesis 12:1-3:

> "And I will make you into a great nation,
> And I will bless you,
> And make your name great;
> And you shall be a blessing;
> And I will bless those who bless you,
> And the one who curses you I will curse.
> And in you all the families of the earth will be blessed."

Genesis 15 records a sacrificial ceremony confirming the covenant. It was a one-way covenant by God, who (while Abraham was asleep) cut the sacrifice in half and walked through alone. The symbolism of this ancient covenantal ceremony essentially communicated, "I am making this promise. If I don't keep it, may I be cut in pieces like this sacrifice." In short, this was an unconditional, binding, permanent covenant God promised to keep.

GENESIS 12:2-3
ONE WAY COVENANT

In Genesis 17:9-14, God added circumcision as a sign of the covenant that Abraham and his descendants were to take. God also changed Abram's name from Abram ("exalted father") to Abraham ("father of a multitude"). Various iterations of the covenant in Genesis—as well as God's initial call of Abram in 12:1—also included specific details about the land. Notice the key details highlighted in the following verses:

> Now the LORD said to Abram,
> "Go from your country,
> And from your relatives
> And from your father's house,
> To *the land* which I will show you."
> (Genesis 12:1, emphasis added)

> "*All the land* which you see I will give to you and to your descendants forever." (Genesis 13:15, emphasis added)

> On that day the LORD made a covenant with Abram, saying,
> "To your descendants I have *given this land,*
> *From the river of Egypt as far as the great river, the river Euphrates.*"
> (Genesis 15:18, emphasis added)

It is extremely important to note that Scripture also clearly foretold that Israel would go through a period of drifting and rebellion that would result in their worldwide dispersion—but afterward God would gather the Jewish people back to their original land. Deuteronomy 30:1-10 details this prophecy with great specificity. For example, in verse 5 we read, "The LORD your God will bring you into *the land which your fathers possessed,* and you shall possess it; and He will be good to you and make you more numerous than your fathers" (emphasis added).

This prophecy has been literally fulfilled, further confirming its legitimacy and permanence. God's covenant was repeated to Abraham's son Isaac, and then again to his grandson Jacob, whose name God changed to *Israel.* Eventually Joshua led the Israelites to take possession of the promised land. Throughout the Old Testament, God's covenant with Abraham clearly and consistently concerned both the people and the land.

As the initial covenant statement in Genesis 12:2-3 predicted, the whole world has truly been blessed through Abraham and his descendants in many ways, not the least of which is the fact that the Scriptures (100 percent of the Old and New Testaments) and the Savior came from the descendants of Abraham. The negative details of the covenant have also proven true. Every enemy who has come against Israel in ancient and modern times has suffered negative consequences.

#7 What Is the Davidic Covenant?

In addition to the broad sweeping Abrahamic covenant concerning both the land and the people, God also made an unconditional and permanent covenant with David through Nathan the prophet (2 Samuel 7). The main features of the Davidic covenant are that it would be permanent and that a future ruler from David's line would establish a kingdom (7:12) whose throne would be established forever (7:16).

In this prophetic covenant there are both near and far elements, or dual-fulfillment (immediate context and future context) prophecies. The text is talking about David's son Solomon for certain details, but also about a mysterious future descendant—whom we now know is Jesus. The Davidic covenant builds on the first prophecy of a Messiah found in Genesis 3:15 regarding the future "seed of the woman" who would come to crush Satan.

PROPHETIC PROGRESSION = JESUS

ONE WAY

OFFSPRING OF THE WOMAN

ABRAHAMIC COVENANT

DAVIDIC COVENANT

The Davidic covenant is repeated in summary form in 1 Chronicles 17:11-14 and 2 Chronicles 6:16. In hindsight (from the point of view from the cross and the prophecies of the end time) we see that the broader promise refers to the future millennial kingdom.

> "When your days are fulfilled that you must go to be with your fathers, then I will set up one of your descendants after you, who will be from your sons; and I will establish his kingdom. He shall build for Me a house, and I will establish his throne forever. I will be his father and he shall be My son; and I will not take my favor away from him, as I took it from him who was before you. But I will settle him in My house and in My kingdom forever, and his throne will be established forever" (1 Chronicles 17:11-14).

The Davidic covenant provides key details that support the logical need for a literal future kingdom run by the Messiah. Further details (particularly in the Psalms, Isaiah, Zechariah, and Revelation 20:1-7) also dictate the logical need for a literal future kingdom. Isaiah 9:6, often read at Christmastime, prophesied the birth of the Messiah—but people often miss that it also says, "The government will rest on His shoulders." So, while there was a gap in the throne (hinted at in 2 Chronicles 6:16), the unconditional promise of an unending future ruler from David's line will find its ultimate fulfillment in the future millennial kingdom (Revelation 20:1-7), and finally in the eternal state (Revelation 21–22).

#8 Do Jewish People Have to Accept Christ to Be Saved?

Yes. Scripture is very clear that everyone must make a personal decision to follow Christ in order to be saved. While the Jews are God's chosen people (based on the Abrahamic covenant, the Davidic covenant, and many specific prophecies about end-time events), they are not automatically saved. They are just automatically preserved as a people, set apart for the fulfillment of God's future plans. In terms of salvation, everyone who is able must personally choose Christ as Savior when presented with the gospel in order to have their sins forgiven. Note the following verses:

> Acts 4:12—There is salvation in no one else; for there is no other name under heaven that has been given among mankind by which we must be saved.

> Romans 3:23-24—All have sinned and fall short of the glory of God, being justified as a gift by His grace through the redemption which is in Christ Jesus.

In Romans chapters 9–11, Paul goes into great detail to answer this question. Notice in the following verses that he clearly states that even God's chosen people must believe on Christ to be saved:

> Romans 10:1-4—Brothers and sisters, my heart's desire and my prayer to God for them is for their salvation. For I testify about them that they have a zeal for God, but not in accordance with knowledge. For not knowing about God's righteousness and seeking to establish their own, they did not subject themselves to the righteousness of God. For Christ is the end of the law for righteousness to everyone who believes.

Notice how clearly Paul shows that Jesus fulfilled the law and that "everyone" must believe on Him to be saved. Also, keep in mind that the fulfillment of the law does not nullify the Abrahamic covenant. God's unconditional and permanent promises to Abraham and his descendants came long before the law was given.

These verses and many others make it abundantly clear that, though God has distinct programs and end-time roles for the Jewish people and the church, each individual must make a personal choice to receive Christ for salvation. In the Old Testament, people looked forward to the coming Messiah. In the church age, we look back to the finished work of Christ on the cross. In the future we will celebrate the moment when Israel's partial blindness is removed and they will finally embrace Jesus as their individual Savior and corporate King.

BEFORE THE CROSS
BELIEVERS LOOKED FORWARD

CHURCH AGE
BELIEVERS LOOK BACK

#9 How Should Christians View the Israeli-Palestinian Conflict?

Prior to 1948, the term *Palestinian* was simply a regional term, not an ethnic term. After Rome destroyed Jerusalem in AD 70, the Jewish people revolted one more time in what is known as the Bar Kokhba revolt (AD 132–135). Around this same time, the Roman emperor Hadrian changed the name of the Judean province. He merged it with the Roman province of Syria and (as an intentional offense to the Jews) renamed it after their ancient archenemies—the Philistines—even though the Philistines no longer existed. The combined name of the province became Syria Palaestina.

During the centuries that followed, various nomadic people groups came and went, but the land was so desolate that very few stayed. Between AD 70 and 1948, *Palestine* became a term that designated a region of the Middle East, but never (in any way) became a sovereign state or had any specific ethnic connection to any people group. People in the region at that time considered themselves Syrians.

In the fourteenth century the area became part of the Ottoman Empire—and remained so until the Ottoman Turks picked the wrong side of WWI, resulting in the dismantling of the empire via the League of Nations' "Mandate for Palestine" (as in the region of Palestine) in July of 1922.

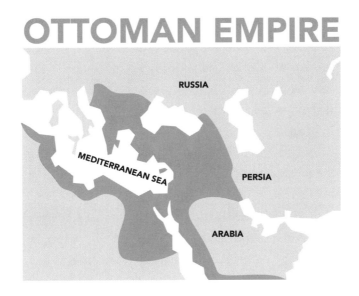

Part of this included the plan to facilitate the establishment of a national home for the Jewish people. A few short months later, the original size of the land planned for the Jewish people was cut by 75 percent. Modern-day Jordan was originally planned as part of the Jewish state, but Arab pressure led to the change in plans. In other words, the separate state that many nations, leaders, and UN resolutions have been pushing for already exists. Jordan was established specifically for the Arabs (whom people now call Palestinians) to have a homeland.

After the horrific events of WWII, in a brief moment of sympathy, the United Nations adopted the resolution to partition Palestine on November 29, 1947. Britain made it known that its oversight of the area would end on

May 15, 1948. So on May 14, 1948, the state of Israel was officially born on a single day exactly as prophesied in Scripture (Isaiah 66:8).

From 1948 until the Six-Day War of 1967, the areas known as the West Bank and Gaza were under the control of Jordan. Never was there any attempt to create a Palestinian state. The Palestine Liberation Organization (PLO) was formed for the express purpose of exterminating the Jewish state. The real goal of the PLO is not the establishment of a Palestinian state—it is the destruction of Israel. The founding charter of the PLO does not recognize Israel's right to exist in any form. That is why no "peace agreement" attempt has ever been accepted by the PLO.

All of this has to do with end-time events and a satanically led hatred for the Jewish people. It really has nothing to do with an oppressed people longing for their own state where they can thrive. In fact, the Arabs who live freely in Israel do thrive. The Arabs under Palestinian leadership (which are actually terrorist groups) suffer greatly and rarely receive any funds or aid from the outside world—unless it is given as a retirement package to the families of terrorists who die trying to kill Jewish people.

With all of that said, we should keep in mind that all people groups in the Middle East should be cared for and treated with respect and dignity. We should pray for God to bless the Arabs/Palestinians as well as the Jewish people. All people are created in the image of God. The commandment by Jesus to love our neighbors as ourselves (Mark 12:31) extends to every people group in every geographic area. There are many Christian ministries in and around Israel with that goal in mind.

#10 Will All Jewish People One Day Turn to Christ?

Yes, at the end of the tribulation period all of the surviving Jewish people will see Christ as their true Messiah and receive Him for salvation. The past few decades have witnessed an ever-growing number of Messianic Jewish

(Jewish people who become Christians) congregations in Israel and around the world.

If there were any question about whether God was finished with His chosen people, Paul very clearly says: "I say then, God has not rejected His people, has He? Far from it! For I too am an Israelite, a descendant of Abraham, of the tribe of Benjamin" (Romans 11:1).

Then later in the same chapter, he doubles down and makes it very clear in verses 25-26, where he says, "I do not want you, brothers and sisters, to be uninformed of this mystery—so that you will not be wise in your own estimation—that a partial hardening has happened to Israel until the fullness of the Gentiles has come in; and so all Israel will be saved."

This does not mean that every Jewish person who has ever lived is automatically saved. It means a time is coming when all of Israel—all remaining Jews—will corporately turn to the Lord for salvation.

When the Jewish religious leaders and the crowds rejected Jesus at His first coming and began their period of partial blindness (as Paul puts it), Jesus stated the following in Matthew 23:37-39,

> "Jerusalem, Jerusalem, who kills the prophets and stones those who are sent to her! How often I wanted to gather your children together, the way a hen gathers her chicks under her wings, and you were unwilling. Behold, your house is being left to you desolate! For I say to you, from now on you will not see Me until you say, 'Blessed is the One who comes in the name of the Lord!'"

The Jewish people (corporately) will not see Jesus until they realize He was the true Savior after all and will call upon Him to save them. We know from Bible prophecy that this will occur at the very end of the seven-year tribulation period also known as Daniel's Seventieth Week (from Daniel 9).

The purpose of the future seven-year tribulation period is primarily to win God's people back to Himself. The majority of the Jewish people will reject Christ as Messiah and embrace a future false messiah (the Antichrist), thinking he is the long-awaited political savior. At the midpoint of the tribulation period, this false messiah will turn on the Jewish people and try to destroy them. He will almost succeed, leaving only a remnant who will be protected and will all call upon Jesus for salvation. You can read about this in Matthew 24 and Revelation 12.

CHAPTER 6

THE TRIBULATION PERIOD

#1 Foretold in the Old Testament

We first learn about the future tribulation period in the Old Testament. It is known by a few names such as the day of the Lord, the time of Jacob's trouble, that day, and the day. Depending on the context, the writers would either be referring to the tribulation period or the tribulation period and the millennial kingdom that will follow it. Sometimes the term is used to indicate God's judgment on a nation in general. Most often the terms are used to describe the end-time period of God's judgment of the earth, commonly called *the tribulation period*.

In Daniel 9:20-27, we learn about a set of seventy "sevens." This is widely understood to be sets of seven years—similar to how we use *decade* for a set of ten years. In Daniel 9:27, we learn that the final set of seven years will feature "the end that is decreed" (NIV). This passage gives us the duration of the future tribulation period (seven years) and the key event that begins the period (the confirming of an agreement between Israel and "many" by an evil end-time ruler).

Many of the Old Testament prophets wrote about this future period of God's intense judgment of the earth. For example, in Isaiah 13:9, we read,

> Behold, the day of the LORD is coming,
> Cruel, with fury and burning anger,

To make the land a desolation;
And He will exterminate its sinners from it.

In Jeremiah 30, we learn that the day of the Lord will come after Israel becomes a nation again (which occurred in 1948). In verse 3, we read, "'Behold, days are coming,' declares the LORD, 'when I will restore the fortunes of My people Israel and Judah.' The LORD says, 'I will also bring them back to the land that I gave to their forefathers, and they shall take possession of it.'"

Then we read this description in verses 5-7:

"For this is what the LORD says:
'I have heard a sound of terror,
Of fear, and there is no peace.
Ask now, and see
If a male can give birth.
Why do I see every man
With his hands on his waist, as a woman in childbirth?
And why have all faces turned pale?
Woe, for that day is great,
There is none like it;
And it is the time of Jacob's distress,
Yet he will be saved from it.'"

We learn from that passage that a main feature of the future tribulation period is that it will be very difficult on Israel (Jacob), but that Israel's ultimate salvation will come out of it. This lines up with additional details we learn about the Jewish people turning to Jesus at the end of the tribulation period. (See question 10 in chapter 5, "Will All Jewish People One Day Turn to Christ?")

Jeremiah continues his description of this future time of calamity. In verses 23-24 we read,

Behold, the tempest of the LORD!
Wrath has gone forth,

A sweeping tempest;
It will whirl upon the head of the wicked.
The fierce anger of the LORD will not turn back
Until He has performed and accomplished
The intent of His heart.
In the latter days you will understand this.

There are dozens of additional passages in the Old Testament prophets that describe the day of the Lord.

VARIOUS TITLES FOR THE DAY OF THE LORD

Jacob's trouble	(Jeremiah 30:7)
Daniel's 70th week	(Daniel 9:24-27)
A time of distress	(Daniel 12:1)
The great day	(Revelation 6:17)
The hour of testing	(Revelation 3:10)
The indignation	(Isaiah 26:20)
Tribulation/great tribulation	(Matthew 24:9, 21, 29; Mark 13:19, 24; Rev 7:14)
The Day of the Lord	(Joel 1:15; 2:1; 1 Thess 5:2)

The characteristics of the day of the Lord as foretold in various Old Testament passages, including those cited above, is that it will be the worst time of judgment the earth will ever see; it will be worse than any other time period in history; it will come suddenly and unexpectedly to those who get caught in it; and it will occur fairly soon after Israel becomes a prosperous nation again.

The tiny country of Israel was reborn in 1948. It is about the size of New Jersey and could fit into Lake Michigan with room to spare—yet it is the eighth most powerful country in the world and its wealth and population continue to grow rapidly. Prophecy is being fulfilled right on track and the long-prophesied day of the Lord is on the near horizon.

With the basic knowledge about the tribulation period provided in the Old Testament (including the start, the duration, a key midpoint event, and the key end-time figure it is centered around), we find more details in the New Testament that help us further understand this future time of judgment.

We learn in 2 Thessalonians 2 that the Antichrist will not rise to power until after the church is removed from the earth via the rapture. We learn additional and mirror details about the tribulation period from Jesus' end-time talk (the Olivet Discourse found in Matthew 24, Mark 13, and Luke 21)—most notably the abomination of desolation. This is the same mid-tribulation event Daniel prophesied about in Daniel 9:27.

Of course, the most prophetic book of the Bible—the book of Revelation—provides the most detail regarding the future seven-year tribulation period. Revelation chapters 6–19 provide a chronological (for the most part) play-by-play description of exactly what will happen during that time.

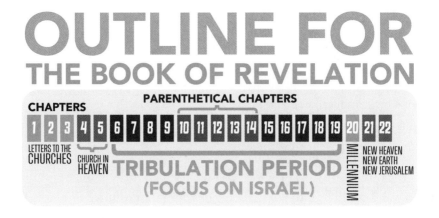

OUTLINE FOR
THE BOOK OF REVELATION

PARENTHETICAL CHAPTERS

CHAPTERS

1 2 3 4 5 6 7 8 9 10 11 12 13 14 15 16 17 18 19 20 21 22

LETTERS TO THE CHURCHES | CHURCH IN HEAVEN | TRIBULATION PERIOD (FOCUS ON ISRAEL) | MILLENNIUM | NEW HEAVEN NEW EARTH NEW JERUSALEM

Like the Old Testament passages, the New Testament also portrays this time of judgment as coming suddenly and unexpectedly—but not to everyone. Those who are watching carefully will be able to "see the day drawing near" (Hebrews 10:25). We learn more about this phenomenon in 1 Thessalonians 5. Many people reference verses 1-2 about the day of the Lord coming like a thief, but they fail to read the next few verses. Read the full passage below carefully.

> Now as to the periods and times, brothers and sisters, you have no need of anything to be written to you. For you yourselves know full well that the day of the Lord is coming just like a thief in the night. While they are saying, "Peace and safety!" then sudden destruction will come upon them like labor pains upon a pregnant woman, and they will not escape. But you, brothers and sisters, are not in darkness, so that the day would overtake you like a thief; for you are all sons of light and sons of day. We are not of night nor of darkness; so then, let's not sleep as others do, but let's be alert and sober (1 Thessalonians 5:1-6).

The passage above details two groups of people. First, we have those who are in the dark, sleeping, and are caught by surprise. Second, we have brothers and sisters who are of the light and children of the day, and who are not caught by surprise. A quick study of the Greek words sheds even more light on these two groups.

The Greek words used for the group that is awake/not caught by surprise are *adelphoi* and *uioi* (literally, "brother" and "son"). These are those (both male and female) who are in the family of God.

The Greek word used for the "others" (i.e., "let's not sleep as others do") is *loipoi* (literally, "the rest/remaining"). The root word of *loipoi* is *leipó* and literally means "to leave behind." This further supports the position of the pretribulation rapture. When we do a little digging, we find there are two distinct groups—the brothers and sisters who will not be caught by surprise by the tribulation period (because they won't be here), and the group that is left behind and caught by surprise.

To Judge the World

While God is abundantly patient and has done everything possible to redeem humanity, He must also—at some point—fully punish sin. Scripture teaches this will happen corporately on earth during a horrific seven-year period (aka the tribulation period; the day of the Lord; the time of Jacob's trouble, Daniel's seventieth week), and individually at the last judgment (aka the great white throne judgment [John 5:28-29; Revelation 20:11-15]).

The tribulation period will come at the end of the church age when evil will have grown to a level where it must be dealt with once and for all. It is important to note God's wrath never falls on those whose sin has already been covered (Luke 21:34-36; 1 Thessalonians 5:9-10; Revelation 3:10). That is why the church will be taken *out of* (Greek word, *ek* [used in Revelation 3:10]) the world (via the rapture) prior to the start of the future tribulation period.

We have two compelling examples in the Old Testament that demonstrate the pattern of God's judgment—the flood of Noah's day and the destruction of Sodom and Gomorrah. In both cases, violence and immorality had grown so much that the only option was judgment. In both cases, God removed the righteous before judgment fell. Jesus referenced both judgments in the Olivet Discourse (Matthew 24:37-39; Luke 17:26-29) and said, "It will be just the same on the day that the Son of Man is revealed" (Luke 17:30).

The level of sin will have reached such a level that even after two sets of horrific judgments in the future tribulation period, many people will still not turn from their wickedness (Revelation 9:20-21).

To Judge the Nations

After the tower of Babel, when God scattered the people and set up nations, He chose Israel as His own. In the Abrahamic covenant, found primarily in Genesis 12:2-3, God said in no uncertain terms that He would bless those who blessed Israel and curse those who cursed Israel. In the end times there will be (and currently is) an obsession with dividing Israel's land, and the nations will be judged for this (Joel 3:1-2; Zechariah 12:2-3) and for general rebellion against God.

The crescendo of this development will occur toward the end of the future tribulation period when *all* the nations of the world gather to prepare for battle against Israel in what is commonly referred to as the battle of (though really a full war campaign) Armageddon (Revelation 16:13-16).

We pick up on this scene again in Revelation 19 where we read this vivid and unpleasant description about the final state of the nations: "I saw the beast and the kings of the earth and their armies, assembled to make war against Him who sat on the horse, and against His army...And the rest were killed with the sword which came from the mouth of Him who sat on the horse, and all the birds were filled with their flesh" (vv. 19,21). We see vignettes of this future scene in the Old Testament as in Psalm 110:6,

> He will judge among the nations,
> He will fill them with corpses,
> He will shatter the chief men over a broad country.

To Punish Satan

Another key purpose of the future tribulation period is to take back the earth from the current unrighteous landlord. Somehow, the fall of mankind caused the earth to come under the rulership of Satan (2 Corinthians 4:3-4). It is interesting to note that the first set of judgments in Revelation

REBELLED IN HEAVEN
CONFINED TO EARTH/PRINCE OF THE POWER OF THE AIR

FUTURE MID-TRIB BATTLE
WILL BE CAST DOWN TO EARTH'S SURFACE

FUTURE DEFEAT
WILL BE BOUND FOR 1,000 YEARS

FUTURE ETERNAL PUNISHMENT
WILL BE CAST INTO THE LAKE OF FIRE FOREVER

SATAN

depict Jesus opening the title deed to the earth to initiate the process of reclaiming it.

Somehow God's decrees and principles have required Satan to be punished in stages instead of immediately judging him. Of course all of this is in accordance with God's ultimate sovereignty and foreordained plans.

To Win Back the Jewish People

Finally, another key purpose of the future seven-year tribulation period is to win God's chosen people back to Himself. The majority of the Jewish people will reject Christ as Messiah and embrace a future false messiah (the Antichrist), thinking he will be the long-awaited political savior. At the midpoint of the future tribulation period, this false messiah will turn on the Jewish people and attempt to completely destroy them. He will almost succeed, leaving only a remnant of Jewish people who will be supernaturally protected and will all corporately call upon Jesus for salvation. You can read about this in Matthew 24 and Revelation 12.

#4 What Are the Gap-Period Events?

Since the confirming of a covenant (Daniel 9:27) is what officially begins the tribulation period, there is a necessary gap between the rapture and the start of the tribulation period. This period will likely be a few weeks to a few months (although Scripture does not provide an exact timeframe). These are some events that will occur in this brief interim period between the rapture and the start of the tribulation period.

Economic and Societal Collapse

At the moment of the rapture, chaos will immediately engulf the world as suddenly unmanned planes, trains, and automobiles crash, and as millions go missing. With the restraining influence of the Holy Spirit and the church now out of the picture, evil will capitalize on this long-awaited set of circumstances. Additionally, the global economy will collapse as a result of the rapture and other events.

4 KEY GAP-PERIOD EVENTS

- **Economic & societal collapse**
- **Globalism achieved**
- **Ezekiel 38 war**
- **Rise of the Antichrist**

Globalism Achieved

Out of this chaos will emerge the long-planned global government and a cashless financial system—both prophesied and required for tribulation events to occur.

Ezekiel 38 War

This may also be the opportune moment for Russia, Iran, and Turkey to lead the prophesied Ezekiel 38 war against Israel. We're not told the exact timing of this future war other than the fact it will be during the last days, when a reborn nation of Israel dwells securely. The chaos, instability, and power vacuum caused by the rapture will surely lead various evil world leaders to pounce on this once-in-a-lifetime opportunity to expand their powers. Like rioters looting unprotected corner stores, unrestrained evil rulers will leverage the lawless chaos to implement their long-laid plans for global domination.

Rise of the Antichrist

The post-rapture global government will give rise to the evil end-time world ruler known as the Antichrist. Scripture teaches that this evil character will emerge from among a set of ten end-time rulers. He will be given great military power such as the world has never known. This charismatic future world leader will rise on the promises of peace, but he will turn out to be the most evil world leader of history. (For more information see chapter 7, "The Antichrist.")

#5 Who Are the Key Figures?

Gog

Ezekiel 38–39 detail a future end-time war against Israel by a coalition of nations that do not border the land of Israel. This future attack will be led by Russia, Iran, and Turkey (joined by a few more nations, including Libya and the Sudan) and will come from Israel's northern border (i.e., from Syria). Gog is the name of the Russian ruler. It is a title like czar or king. Some prophecy experts also cite the possibility that Gog may be the name of a demon who is behind the Russian ruler. Gog is seen in the Ezekiel account as the main leader—a protector of sorts to the other partners. His main motive will be to take plunder from Israel (most likely gas, oil, and other natural resources) at a time of vulnerability (most likely immediately following the rapture).

Antichrist

The *anti* in Antichrist has a double meaning. It means "in place of," and it also means "against." So, the Antichrist will be a false messiah who is coming against the true Messiah—Jesus Christ. This evil end-time ruler will arise out of the post-rapture chaos (most likely from Western Europe based on Daniel 9:26). He will then confirm (strengthen/finalize) a covenant with Israel (Daniel 9:27). When the ink dries, the seven-year tribulation period will officially begin. At the midpoint of the tribulation he will be possessed by Satan, will break his covenant and turn on the Jewish people, leading to a second (and much worse) holocaust. He and the false prophet will institute the mark of the beast and will behead anyone who refuses. He will be defeated by Christ at the end of the tribulation period—thrown alive into the lake of fire.

False Prophet

The false prophet's role will be to point people to the Antichrist, mimicking how the Holy Spirit points people to Jesus. The Antichrist, the false prophet, and Satan will form a counterfeit trinity of sorts. Revelation 13:11 depicts this figure having two horns like a lamb but the voice of a dragon. He will seem to be a gentle religious figure but will actually speak satanic lies. After the rapture, the false prophet will amalgamate the world religions into one global religion. Then at the midpoint of the tribulation period he will help enforce the mark of the beast and the worship of the Antichrist.

The 144,000

This large group of Jewish witnesses will emerge somewhere in the first half of the future tribulation period. We first learn of them in Revelation 7:4. God will sovereignly choose 12,000 from each tribe to be sealed for a special witnessing ministry. They are the first fruits (Revelation 14:4) of Jewish people who will receive Christ in the tribulation period. Their powerful ministry will help lead millions (perhaps billions) to Christ after the rapture (Revelation 7:9). Revelation 14:1-5 describes them as standing with Christ on Mount Zion singing a new song that only they will know. This could mean they will be martyred, or it could simply be a flash-forward to the end of the tribulation period.

The Two Witnesses

The two witnesses will appear sometime after the rapture but before the very beginning of the tribulation period. They will prophesy for 1,260 days—which comes out to three-and-a-half years (using Israel's 360-day year model). We are told that they will be able to breathe fire and destroy people who try to harm them, turn off the rain, turn water into blood, and "strike the earth with every plague, as often as they desire" (Revelation 11:6). These end-time superheroes will undoubtedly capture the attention of the world during the first three-and-a-half years of the tribulation period.

At the midpoint of the tribulation they will be killed by the Antichrist (referred to here as the beast) to everyone's surprise and delight. The world will celebrate their deaths (Revelation 11:9-10), but the celebrating will be premature. After three-and-a-half days the two witnesses will be resurrected and raptured before a watching world.

NEWS | **SIGN OF THE TIMES**

NEWS CAN BE SEEN INSTANTLY AND GLOBALLY

The two witnesses will most likely be Moses and Elijah, although other popular candidates are the apostle John and Enoch. Moses and Elijah traditionally represent the law and the prophets. They were also the two who showed up in Matthew 17 when Jesus was momentarily changed into His glorified version in front of Peter, James, and John. The miraculous signs the two witnesses will be able to perform mirror those of Moses and Elijah.

Moses and Elijah also both had unique exits. Moses died and was buried by God Himself (Deuteronomy 34) under very mysterious circumstances where Satan attempted to take the body of Moses (Jude 9). Elijah was taken up to heaven without dying via a tornado-driven team of fiery horses

(2 Kings 2:11-12). An argument could even be made that since Moses died and Elijah was taken without dying, this displays how the law has been fulfilled or completed, but prophecy has not yet been fully fulfilled.

#6 What Starts the Tribulation?

While many assume the rapture is the event that will begin the tribulation, the confirming of a covenant will be the detail that officially begins the tribulation period. In Daniel 9:27, we read, "He will confirm a covenant with the many for one week, but in the middle of the week he will put a stop to sacrifice and grain offering; and on the wing of abominations will come the one who makes desolate, until a complete destruction, one that is decreed, gushes forth on the one who makes desolate."

We also read this in Revelation 6:1-2, "Then I saw when the Lamb broke one of the seven seals, and I heard one of the four living creatures saying as with a voice of thunder, 'Come!' I looked, and behold, a white horse, and the one who sat on it had a bow; and a crown was given to him, and he went out conquering and to conquer."

KEY DETAILS OF
THE TRIBULATION PERIOD

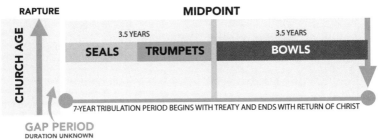

	RAPTURE	MIDPOINT	
CHURCH AGE	3.5 YEARS	3.5 YEARS	
	SEALS TRUMPETS	BOWLS	

7-YEAR TRIBULATION PERIOD BEGINS WITH TREATY AND ENDS WITH RETURN OF CHRIST

GAP PERIOD
DURATION UNKNOWN

We understand from Daniel 2 and 7 and Revelation 13 and 17 that the rider on the white horse is none other than the Antichrist. This evil end-time ruler will be a false messiah and will appear on the scene after the rapture. The event that will officially begin the seven-year tribulation (and clearly identify the Antichrist) will be the confirming of a treaty led by this new, seemingly peaceful ruler. He will arise out of a ten-nation confederacy from the region that used to be part of the ancient Roman Empire (see Daniel 2:42; 7:24; Revelation 13:1-2).

Once the ink dries on the treaty papers, Daniel's seventieth week (Daniel 9:27) will begin and the exact seven-year countdown to the return of Christ to set up the millennial kingdom will begin.

#7 What Are the Seal Judgments?

The seal judgments will be the first set of seven (out of twenty-one total) judgments that will occur in the future tribulation period. The first four of the seal judgments make up the well-known four horsemen of the apocalypse.

THE SEAL JUDGMENTS

1. WHITE HORSE
2. RED HORSE
3. BLACK HORSE
4. PALE HORSE
5. MARTYRDOM
6. EARTHQUAKE
7. PRELUDE

Seal Judgment 1: The Rider on the White Horse (Revelation 6:1-2)

This evil end-time ruler will be a false messiah and will appear on the scene after the rapture. He will arise out of a ten-nation/elite-ruler confederacy from what was formerly part of the ancient Roman Empire (see Daniel 2:42; 7:24; Revelation 13:1-2), and he will confirm a covenant with Israel to begin the tribulation period.

Seal Judgment 2: The Red Horse (Revelation 6:3-4)

At the breaking of the second seal, peace will be taken from the earth. This could mean that the plethora of regional conflicts and threats of war that are bubbling beneath the surface in our day finally erupt into a larger global war. Or it could mean the Antichrist will (in his quest for global rule) take peace from the earth as he begins to conquer the unwilling by military force.

Seal Judgment 3: The Black Horse (Revelation 6:5-6)

The logical outcome of world war is famine. As food distribution systems break down, riots shut down cities, electronic systems fail, and crops and factories are destroyed by war—the worst famine the world has ever seen will lead to the death of multitudes.

Seal Judgment 4: The Pale Horse (Revelation 6:7-8)

The fourth seal introduces the pale horse of death. The conditions resulting from the first three seals lead to massive death as war, famine, plague, and "beasts of the earth" (possibly including viruses) will cause one-quarter of the world's population to die.

Seal Judgment 5: Martyrdom (Revelation 6:9-11)

In the wake of the rapture, history will witness the largest single great awakening as large numbers turn to Christ. As people look for answers they will find Bibles and resources left behind, and experience the ministry of the 144,000 and the two witnesses. But the globalist agenda of the elite and the Antichrist will not be stopped. The gloves will come off, and anyone found to have become a believer in Christ will be severely persecuted and martyred in quick fashion.

Seal Judgment 6: Global Mega-Quake (Revelation 6:12-17)

The sixth seal judgment will literally rock the world to its core. It appears that during this judgment, many of the earth's fault lines will fracture and a catastrophic global earthquake will trigger volcanoes. The worldwide eruptions will blacken the sky. At the same time, a massive meteor or asteroid event will occur.

Seal Judgment 7: Prelude to the Next Set of Judgments

After the account of the sealing of the 144,000 in Revelation 7, John describes the breaking of the seventh and final seal in chapter 8. The final seal judgment will initiate a dramatic pause that will set up the next set of global calamities, known as the trumpet judgments. It's important to note that the seventh judgment in each of the sets of seven judgments (seals, trumpets, bowls) unlocks the next phase of judgment and includes a proclamation (or strange silence in the case of the seventh seal), thunder, lightning, something falling from the sky, and increasingly destructive earthquakes.

#8 What Are the Trumpet Judgments?

The second set of judgments in the future tribulation period are known as the trumpet judgments.

They are as follows:

Trumpet Judgment 1: Hail, Fire, and Blood from the Sky

With the first trumpet judgment we find that one-third of the forests and vegetation will be destroyed and all grass on the earth will be destroyed. The earth will be scorched.

THE TRUMPET
JUDGMENTS
1 HAIL, FIRE, BLOOD
2 BURNING MOUNTAIN
3 STAR WORMWOOD
4 SUN DIMINISHED
5 DEMONIC LOCUSTS
6 DEMONIC HORSEMEN
7 PRELUDE

Trumpet Judgment 2: Flaming "Mountain" Landing in the Ocean

With the second trumpet judgment, John depicts "something like a great mountain burning with fire" (Revelation 8:8) being thrown into the sea. A celestial object will land in the ocean, and the ensuing tsunamis and devastation will destroy one-third of the sea life and one-third of the ships in the ocean.

Trumpet Judgment 3: A Great Falling Star Poisons Water Sources

The third trumpet will bring another falling celestial object, this time smaller than the previous judgment but just as destructive. According to John, the projectile has a name—Wormwood. We speculate, but it seems that Wormwood may either be a nuclear weapon or a large meteor or asteroid. In any case, it will poison a third of the world's water supply.

Trumpet Judgment 4: Sun, Moon, and Stars Dimmed by One-Third

The logical result of fiery meteor showers, a giant asteroid, and nuclear weapons striking the earth in quick succession would be a partial blackout. As smoke and destruction rise in the air, the heavenly lights created by God to guide mankind will be dimmed to a mere two-thirds of their normal brightness.

Trumpet Judgment 5: Falling "Star" Opens the Abyss (The First Woe)

With the final three trumpet judgments—also called the three woes—we see a new level of paranormal involvement added to the judgments. The first 11 verses of Revelation 9 describe yet another falling star. Unlike the previous falling objects, this one is given personality. It will be given a key, and it is referred to as a "he" in verse 2. This "star" may be Satan himself finally being cast out of heaven. Isaiah may have been speaking about this moment in Isaiah 14:12:

"How you have fallen from heaven,
You star of the morning, son of the dawn!
You have been cut down to the earth,
You who defeated the nations!"

He will be given "the key to the shaft of the abyss" (Revelation 9:1; see also Luke 8:30-31; 2 Peter 2:4; Jude 5-7). Whether this abyss is a physical place beneath the earth's crust or exists in the unseen realm, the key will crack open the barrier, releasing the thick, foul, sky-darkening smoke as a horde of demonic stinging "locusts" pour through. They will be led by a fallen angel named Destroyer (Abaddon in Hebrew or Apollyon in Greek). Perhaps this is Satan, the "fallen star" who was given the ability to open the abyss in the opening verse of Revelation 9. Joel 2:1-11 also describes these terrible creatures that will invade earth during the tribulation period, which Joel and other Old Testament prophets call "the day of the LORD" (2:1,11,31).

Trumpet Judgment 6: Four Killer Angels and the Demonic Army of 200 Million (The Second Woe)

Apparently, right now, there are fallen angels bound in chains (you can read about this in the book of Jude and a few other places in Scripture), reserved for a certain day and purpose. In Revelation 9:13 and following, John tells us about four such angels bound at the Euphrates River. These four fallen angels will lead a demonic horde of 200 million to kill one-third of those alive at that time.

Trumpet Judgment 7: Ushering in the Final Set of Judgments (The Third Woe)

With the seventh trumpet judgment (Revelation 11), John describes the finality that will result from the final bowl judgments that the seventh trumpet unlocks. In other words, the seventh trumpet's main purpose will be to usher in the final phase of the tribulation period characterized by the seven bowl judgments.

It appears that the first two sets of judgments will culminate by the mid-point of the tribulation period where several key events occur before the final set of seven judgments. Here's a list of ten key midtrib events.

The three sets of judgments described in Revelation get progressively worse. In Revelation 16, they are as bad as they get. In previous judgments we saw God holding back, allowing, for example, only one-third of the trees to be destroyed or one-third of the sun to be darkened. Here in John's description of the final bowl judgments, there's no holding back.

10 KEY MID-TRIB EVENTS

1 Antichrist killed
2 Satan cast down to Earth
3 Antichrist "resurrected"
4 Religious Babylon destroyed
5 Abomination of desolation
6 Covenant broken
7 Jews persecuted worldwide
8 Mark of the beast implemented
9 Worship of Antichrist
10 2 witnesses killed

Bowl Judgment 1: Sores

The first bowl judgment results in "harmful and painful sores" on those who will take the mark of the beast. This may have to do with DNA manipulation gone bad, some kind of malfunctioning technical poisoning. Scripture doesn't tell us the cause of the sores, but it seems logical that they will be related to the mark that was received.

Bowl Judgment 2: Ocean Turned to Blood

The second bowl judgment turns the entire ocean into blood, killing everything in it. Can you imagine the worldwide stench! We don't know if it will be literal blood or what is known today as "red tide" where tiny microorganisms multiply rapidly, turning water red and depleting it of oxygen—resulting in the massive death of sea life. It is interesting to note that incidents of "red tide" have been on the rise in recent years.

Bowl Judgment 3: Fresh Water Turned to Blood

The third bowl judgment will have the same effect on the rivers and springs, so every major water source on earth will be polluted. This judgment is reminiscent of one of the judgments Moses leveled on ancient Egypt.

Bowl Judgment 4: Intense Heat

The fourth bowl judgment seems to include a massive breakdown of the earth's atmosphere and massive solar flares or coronal mass ejections. People will be "scorched with fierce heat" from the sun (Revelation 16:9). Yet we are told they will still refuse to repent and glorify God.

Bowl Judgment 5: Darkness

The fifth bowl judgment will plunge the beast's kingdom into darkness. Again, this is similar to a judgment Moses brought upon ancient Egypt when Pharaoh refused to let the Israelites go. People will take their rebellion a step further and curse God.

Bowl Judgment 6: Euphrates Dries Up

The sixth bowl judgment will dry up the Euphrates River "so that the way would be prepared for the kings from the east" (Revelation 16:12). These will be massive armies from Asia, coming to join the final end-time battle described below.

Bowl Judgment 7: The Ultimate Earthquake

The seventh bowl judgment will include the worst earthquake the world has ever seen. The earthquake in the first half of the tribulation moved mountains and islands from their place, indicating a possible pole or crustal shift. The tribulation era's final earthquake will cause entire cities to collapse, Jerusalem to split into three, every island to sink, and every mountain to crumble. If that weren't bad enough, 100-pound hailstones will fall on the armies assembled to fight God.

#10 What Are the Battles of Armageddon?

In the lead-up to the military campaign of Armageddon, Daniel 11:40-45 describes a Middle East military conflict that will occur toward the end of the tribulation period. After the pivotal midtribulation events (described in the previous section), Antichrist will pursue the Jewish people and the multitudes of new believers with intense violence (Revelation 12:13-16; 13:7). It appears that at this same time, some nations of the world attempt to push back against the global rulership of the Antichrist.

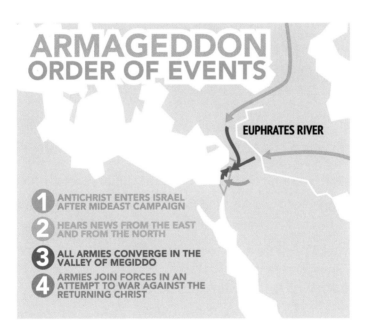

After a successful military campaign in the Middle East, just as he enters the land of Israel, the Antichrist will hear news of from the east and from the north that alarms him. This could mean that Russia will have shored up its military enough to muster an assault (having been decimated in the Ezekiel 38 defeat roughly seven years prior) at the same time the armies of the kings of the east (spoken of in Revelation 16:12) will be about to cross the Euphrates River on their way to confront him. The perfect storm of circumstances will cause all of these armies to converge on the most famous battle staging area of the world—the valley of Megiddo. Better known as Armageddon.

Just as all of the Daniel 11 armies arrive, their attention will suddenly shift in a way that unites them to fight a much greater foe—Jesus Christ. Matthew 24:30 informs us that when the Lord is about to return at the end of the tribulation period, "then the sign of the Son of Man will appear in the sky, and then all the tribes of the earth will mourn, and they will see the Son of Man coming on the clouds of the sky with power and great glory." It seems the armies will see this sign (perhaps God's heavenly shekinah glory piercing the blackness of the global judgment) and know exactly what it means. The Lord will be coming to judge them. The godless armies led by the Antichrist—in their ultimate self-delusion—will think they can actually combine forces to take on the Son of God.

CHAPTER 7

THE ANTICHRIST

#1 Is Antichrist a Real Person?

Some commentators have speculated that Antichrist is not a specific individual at all, but rather a symbol of some end-time world governmental system. Others think the word represents a secret "deep state" committee or even some form of futuristic artificial intelligence. There are those who prefer an even more abstract view, claiming the term *Antichrist* is simply a metaphor for the principle of evil itself. They claim the phrase "*spirit* of the antichrist" (1 John 4:3) demonstrates that he is not a person but more of a metaphysical reality.

In contrast to those views, we believe Antichrist is an actual man who will emerge upon the horizon in history's last days. But how do we come to this conclusion? Keep in mind that your interpretation of Scripture is always determined by the interpretive method you use. If you approach Scripture in a symbolic nonliteral way, you open yourself up to a wide variety of interpretations on any given passage. This is nowhere truer and more dangerous than when it comes to Bible prophecy. In the book of Revelation there are not only many bizarre descriptions of actual events, people, and places but also symbols as well. Fortunately for us, John explains the meanings of many of these symbols and word pictures (Revelation 11:8; 12:1-2,5-6,14; 17:1-7,12,18). However, as previously stated, the safest and most reliable method for interpreting the Bible is to assume that it means what it says, and that the plain sense of a passage, sentence, or word will most likely reveal the original intent of the author.

With this in mind, when it comes to Antichrist, John specifically refers to him by that title five times in his epistles (1 John 2:18 [twice],22; 4:3; 2 John 1:7). Male pronouns are also used to describe him: king, prince (Daniel 8:23; 9:26), man, and son (2 Thessalonians 2:3-4). Further, the following Bible personalities all depict Antichrist as an actual person: Daniel (Daniel 7:8,20,24-25; 8:25; 9:27; 11:21,24,31,36-37), Zechariah (11:15-17), Paul (2 Thessalonians 2:3-4,8-9), John (see above), Jesus (Matthew 24:15, 24), and Revelation's angel (Revelation 17:7). Further, John plainly tells us that the mark of the beast is the number of a *man* (Revelation 13:18).

> Antichrist is an actual man who will emerge during history's last days.

And finally, if Antichrist is not a real person, then how can we be sure that any of the other events or people in the book of Revelation are also actual? This opens up Revelation to unlimited interpretations. Therefore, because of these reasons, we believe Antichrist is a real, flesh-and-blood man.

#2 When and How Will He Be Revealed?

The timing of Antichrist's coming out is critical, and according to Scripture must be preceded by other fulfilled prophecies. For example, in order for Antichrist to fulfill the prophecy of Daniel 9:27 (signing a peace treaty with Israel), Israel must be a nation again and living in the land (Ezekiel 36–37; Isaiah 66:8-9; Jeremiah 16:14-15; 31:3-9). This officially happened on May 14, 1948. Since that time, Jews have been steadily flooding back to Israel from all over the world. Today, more Jews are living in the Holy Land than in any other place on earth.

Second, the apostle Paul tells us that Antichrist cannot be revealed until the "restrainer" is taken out of the way (2 Thessalonians 2:6-8). Though some have speculated that the restrainer refers to government, it makes more sense to see the restrainer as the Holy Spirit. During the tribulation, there will be no more powerful man on the planet than the one possessed by Satan. Therefore, only a spiritual force *greater* than Satan could presently hold back Antichrist with his evil agenda.

And what could possibly trigger the Holy Spirit's restraining influence to be removed from the earth? The rapture is the best explanation for this, because when every Christian in the world is taken up to heaven, there will be no one left to represent, speak up for, or fight for righteousness. This is why verse 7 speaks of the "mystery of lawlessness," referring to Antichrist's blatant disregard for morality and God's standards. Satan's Antichrist will be like a horse in the gate, eager to burst upon the scene and gallop his way into history, promising peace and safety (1 Thessalonians 5:3; Revelation 6:1-2).

BEFORE ANTICHRIST CAN BE REVEALED:

1 ISRAEL REBORN AND LIVING IN LAND — STATUS FULFILLED

2 RESTRAINER REMOVED (RAPTURE) — STATUS NOT YET FULFILLED

The global chaos that results from the rapture's devastation on humanity will create a massive void filled with panic at every level. Entire countries will collapse, thrusting the world's economy into a dark abyss. There will be confusion and upheaval at every segment of society: economically, socially, militarily, politically, medically, and morally. Into this crisis will step the man of Satan's own choosing, having groomed him for this very moment. Historically, populations have accepted promises of hope and change in order to lift them out of despair and emotional darkness. And this post-rapture crisis will be like none other in history. And the greater the need, the greater this false messiah's persona and ego will be. He will be the world's greatest opportunist, and will romance, cajole, and deceive billions to accept him as the man of the hour (2 Thessalonians 2:8-12).

#3 Will Antichrist Be a Jew, Gentile, or Muslim?

Revelation 13 tells us the Antichrist (or "beast," Greek *theron,* meaning "wild, ferocious animal" and used 36 times to refer to Antichrist) will "come up out of the sea." The passage goes on to describe his assent to power and the ten-nation confederacy over which he will preside. However, the key phrase here is "come up out of the sea." To what is John referring? It helps to compare this with Revelation 17:15, where the angel tells John, "the waters which you saw where the prostitute sits are peoples and multitudes, and nations and languages." This "sea" then likely refers to Gentile nations. Another evidence for Antichrist being a Gentile is from Daniel 11:37, where it pictures him as having "no regard for the gods of his fathers." Because of the plural form of this word ("gods"—*elohim*), it is probably not a reference to Judaism or Islam, both monotheistic religions.

Historically, the person who most prefigures Antichrist's character and actions is Antiochus Epiphanes, a Gentile who ruled the Seleucid Empire from 175 BC until 164 BC. When he invaded Jerusalem, he committed an abomination in the Jewish temple, slaughtering a pig in the holy of holies, and also setting up an image of himself in the temple. We know that this abomination by Antiochus is *not* the complete fulfillment of Daniel 9:27, because Jesus Himself predicted this passage would be fulfilled as a *future* event (Matthew 24:15).

Another evidence Antichrist will be a Gentile is that he will rule over a European union comprised of Gentile nations (Daniel 7:19-27). He also is the chief ruler over what Jesus referred to as the "times of the Gentiles" (Luke 21:24), a period where Israel is dominated by Gentile rule. This will continue until she is restored in the millennial kingdom (Revelation 20:1-6). Daniel always puts Antichrist in a close association with what will be a revived Roman Empire, indicating he will have some degree of Roman origin. Daniel prophesied that "the people of the prince who is to come" would destroy Jerusalem and the temple (Daniel 9:26). We know from history that the Romans did this in AD 70. Again, Roman origin, and thus Gentile.

These reasons, along with the continual rise of anti-Semitism in the world, especially leading up to and including the tribulation period, tell us it is unlikely the Antichrist will be a Jew. It is also unlikely a Jew would commit the abomination of desolation, proclaiming himself to be God Almighty in the holy of holies (Daniel 7:25; 2 Thessalonians 2:4; Revelation 11:1-2; 13:6-7).

It is also believed by some that Antichrist will be Muslim. The Quran version of their Messiah (called the Mahdi) bears some eerie similarities to the biblical description of the Antichrist (i.e., he rides a white horse, kills Jews, and reigns for seven years). But we reject this interpretation for three reasons:

1. The already cited evidence for Antichrist being a Gentile.

2. Muhammed, who was illiterate, dictated the Quran to scribes, and his information regarding the end times was loosely based on what he had heard from Christians, Jews, and followers of Zoroastrianism.[33]

3. The highest confession of any Muslim is, "There is no God but Allah." For a Muslim to declare himself to be God (Allah) and to demand the world worship him is an unthinkable concept in Islam.

For these reasons, we believe the Antichrist will be a Gentile.

#4 Why Does Antichrist Hate the Jews So Much?

In Revelation 12, we are told of a pivotal event that takes place in heaven at the midpoint of the tribulation. It's a war, actually. Here, Satan and his demons attempt one final coup on the heavenly throne of God (Isaiah 14:13-14). Having previously had access to God's presence where he brought accusations against believers, this proves to be Satan's final appearance there (Job 1:6-12; 2:1-5; Luke 22:31-32; Revelation 12:10). Michael and his angels wage war with Satan and his demons, defeating them and casting them down to the earth. It is at this point that Satan becomes enraged with a great wrath, a *rampage* wrath, and made even more so because he realizes "he has only a short time" (Revelation 12:12). And so, knowing his time is limited, what does he choose to do?

He relentlessly goes after the Jews in a three-pronged attack. *First*, he begins a deliberate persecution of the Jewish people. Breaking his covenant with them, he enters the third temple and commits the "abomination of desolation," defying the holy of holies, claiming *himself* to be God (Daniel 9:27; Matthew 24:15-22; 2 Thessalonians 2:3-4; Revelation 12:13). It is at this time that the Jews frantically flee into the wilderness, where they are supernaturally protected by God (Revelation 12:14).

Second, Satan unleashes some sort of flood meant to destroy this remnant, but again, God intervenes and protects her (Revelation 12:15-16). Whether this is a literal flood or instead pictures an invading army, we cannot be certain. But what is sure is that Satan is not giving up yet.

Finally, with his blood boiling, the devil becomes enraged with the Jews, launching an all-out military campaign against the remaining believers, possibly including Jew and Gentile (Revelation 12:17). When the dust clears, two-thirds of all Jews will have died (Zechariah 13:8).

But why the Jews? Why does Satan have such a specific hatred for this race of people? *First*, the very first prophecy in Scripture concerning the coming Savior is found in Genesis 3:15, where the seed of the woman bruises the serpent's head. God further elaborated on this promise by telling Abraham, "In you all the families of the earth will be blessed" (Genesis 12:3). So, reason number one why Satan hates the Jews is because through the Jewish Messiah, salvation has come to those held in bondage by the devil.

Second, Satan hates the Jews because the vast majority of Scripture was written by the Hebrews. Without Scripture we would not know and understand the way of salvation or how to give glory to God.

Third, Satan knows that Jesus' second coming will include rescuing the Jewish remnant, and he wants to do everything within his power to prevent them from crying out to their Messiah to save them. If the Jews are dead, then they can't call on Him for salvation. And if they can't do this, theoretically speaking, there won't be a second coming. Therefore, Satan would be able to continue his unchecked reign upon the earth through Antichrist (Isaiah 34:1-7; 63:1-6; Habakkuk 3:3; Micah 2:12-13; Romans 11:25-27).

Christ's return will also signal Satan's ultimate doom. Lucifer's endgame has always been to be God, to be worshiped, and to rule the world. And the Jews and their promised Messiah are all that stand in his way.

THREE REASONS
FOR SATAN'S HATRED
OF THE JEWISH PEOPLE

1 THE MESSIAH CAME THROUGH THE JEWS

2 THE SCRIPTURES CAME THROUGH THE JEWS

3 JESUS WILL RETURN TO RESCUE THE JEWS AND BIND SATAN

#5 What Does Antichrist's Reign Look Like?

Scripture doesn't tell us whether Antichrist will be a previously known politician or if he will rise out of obscurity in the post-rapture chaos. What recent history has taught us, however, is that it is possible for a man to ascend to the pinnacle of political power with limited previous experience. We saw this in America with the meteoric rise and election of Barack Obama, a man out of nowhere, as president. But one of Antichrist's characteristics is that he will be an opportunist who possesses the unique ability to persuade others with his personality and speaking skills (Daniel 8:23-25). Built on a platform of peace and safety, Antichrist begins his political career by brokering a peace treaty with Israel (Daniel 7:25; 8:25; 9:27; 12:7; 1 Thessalonians 5:1-3; Revelation 6:2). He will form a ten-nation coalition that will, in essence, be a revived Roman Empire, described as "ten toes" and "ten horns" (Daniel 2:31-45; 7:19-28; Revelation 12:3; 13:1-9;

17:3,12-13). An empire such as this has never existed, and certainly not as an extension of the ancient Roman Empire.

But how can we be certain that this interpretation is correct? In Daniel 7, the prophet tells us about four empires, which history reveals as Babylon (7:1-4), Medo-Persia (7:5), Greece (7:6), and Rome (7:7-8). He then describes the empire of Rome, which historically followed Greece (7:7). However, he then shifts to describe another form of this empire, one having "ten horns." And why do we believe this is a future version of the Roman Empire? First, it is clearly linked with Rome in verse 7. But second, as mentioned before, Rome never existed in a ten-king state. Third, Daniel 2:34-35 prophesies that this empire will be suddenly crushed by the "stone" of Messiah's kingdom. But the Roman Empire was not suddenly crushed by some other kingdom. Rather, it declined gradually over the course of a thousand years. Therefore, this part of Daniel's prophecy must still be future, and as of right now, unfulfilled.

We also see a dramatic shift in both the character of the Antichrist and the nature of his rule during the seven-year tribulation. At the halfway point of this period of time, he is fully possessed by Satan, becoming much more dictatorial and diabolical.

A second and third characteristic of Antichrist's reign will be addressed in the next question.

#6 What Is "666"?

Two other aspects of Antichrist's reign are characterized as *economic* and *religious*. Scripture claims he will suffer a fatal head wound around the midpoint of the tribulation (Revelation 13:3-4,12,14; 17:8). However, he will rise from the dead, deceiving the world into believing that he is a deity, even claiming himself to be God (Daniel 11:36; 2 Thessalonians 2:3-5,9-12). The nations will fall for this great deception, and due to the catastrophic economic impact the judgments of God have already had on the planet, the masses are willing to surrender their personal liberties, swearing allegiance to Antichrist in exchange for the ability to buy and sell (Revelation 13:16-18).

Much has been said regarding the infamous "mark of the beast" (Revelation 16:2; 19:20) or "666." Let's talk about what it actually is and what it does or provides. First, the Greek word John uses for "mark" is *charagma*, which in his day immediately brought to mind the images or names of Roman emperors found on coins. There were also slaves and soldiers who would take an identifying mark or brand, demonstrating their loyalty to their masters or military commanders.

Second, Scripture is clear that this mark will be applied to one of only two places on the human body—the right hand or the forehead. It also says

the mark will be *on* (Greek, *epi*) the hand or forehead, not *in* it. So, whatever this mark will be, it has to be visibly seen and/or read electronically from the surface of the skin. This *could* refer to an epidermal tattoo or smart tattoo containing financial information.

So what does this mark do or provide? It is possible the wearing of the mark merely gives a person admission into the marketplace whereupon they would be free to use whatever payment method they so desire. It could be the image, outline, or profile of the Antichrist, his name, or the number of his name, which is 666. We will discuss more about the identity of Antichrist in the next question. So, one of its purposes will be to serve as a sort of economic passport, enabling a person to purchase goods and to sell them. However, without the mark, a person will not be able to buy or sell. It will be required in order to be a citizen who participates in the economy.

The final aspect of the mark is religious in nature. Because Antichrist will persuade the world to believe he has risen from the dead, he will also subsequently require everyone to worship him as God. The one who enforces this mandated policy is a second beast known as the false prophet (Revelation 13:11-16). This man makes sure that not only everyone takes the mark, but also that they pay homage to the Antichrist as God. So, unless you worship the Antichrist and take his mark, you risk financial ruin and starvation.

Finally, whoever takes the mark effectively seals their eternal destiny. Scripture is very clear that anyone accepting Antichrist's mark will also taste the wine of the wrath of God and be sentenced to eternal damnation (Revelation 14:9-10; 16:2; 19:20-21). On the other hand, Scripture is equally clear that no true believer will end up taking the mark of the beast (Revelation 20:4).

#7 Is It Possible to Discern the Identity of Antichrist?

Every time a slick politician or evil dictator rises onto the global stage, immediately some begin speculating whether or not he could be "the one," the Antichrist. They do this primarily for three reasons: First, we are living

in the last days; therefore, they conclude, Satan may at times overplay his hand, letting the cat out of the bag (Antichrist's identity) prematurely. Second, when a world leader exhibits characteristics consistent with those of the Antichrist, it causes some to wonder if he could indeed be that prophesied person. And third, some people believe it is possible to mathematically decode Antichrist's identity through the practice of gematria, a method of converting letters to their Hebrew numerical counterparts. In other words, by figuring out the equivalent of a person's name in Hebrew, you can decipher their name numerically. Using this method, 666 has been linked to everyone from John Kennedy to Ronald Reagan to Barack Obama.

However, we believe it is impossible to definitively identify the Antichrist right now for three very important reasons. First, the context of Revelation 13:18 refers to those living during the time of Antichrist's mark (during the tribulation). It is to this "tribulation generation" that John gives the hint of wisdom and calculating the number of the beast. Second, Scripture seems to indicate that the Antichrist will not be known *until* he makes a peace covenant with Israel (Daniel 9:27). From a strategy standpoint, it would be foolish for Satan to allow the identity of the Antichrist to be known ahead of his grand reveal. Doing that would certainly be anticlimactic, weakening the impact of

To claim knowledge of Antichrist's identity right now is to flatly contradict Scripture.

his public persona. Third, the Bible also says he will not be revealed until *after* the rapture (2 Thessalonians 2:6-8). So, to claim knowledge of Antichrist's identity right now is to flatly contradict Scripture.

Even so, we have been approached on multiple occasions by people who say they know who Antichrist is based on some secret information they have obtained through direct revelation from God. The bad news is, according to the Bible, if they did actually know who Antichrist was, they would've missed the rapture and been left behind!

#8 What Is the "Spirit of the Antichrist"?

This phrase is found in 1 John 4:3, and at its core means "every spirit that does not confess Jesus is not from God; this is the spirit of the antichrist, which you have heard is coming, and now it is already in the world."

Keep in mind that the *anti* in Antichrist means "in place of" and "against." So, the spirit of antichrist, broadly speaking, applies to any spirit (thought, teaching, philosophy, movement) that refuses to acknowledge Jesus Christ as God. Second John 1:7 echoes this truth, "For many deceivers have gone out into the world, those who do not acknowledge Jesus Christ as coming in the flesh. This is the deceiver and the antichrist." This is why John urged us to "test the spirits to see whether they are from God" (1 John 4:1). John also says that even in his day, "many antichrists have appeared," and that this was one of the signs that we are living in the "last hour" (1 John 2:18).

> The spirit of antichrist, broadly speaking, applies to any spirit (thought, teaching, philosophy, movement) that refuses to acknowledge Jesus Christ as God.

The final (and actual) Antichrist will do everything possible, using the power Satan has given him, to publicly deny the true nature of Jesus Christ. He will substitute himself for Christ, becoming a false messiah. This is exactly what Jesus warns those tribulation disciples about. In one of His final messages to His disciples, He deals exclusively with the subject of the end times, specifically the tribulation. When they ask Him about the timing of those events and the signs that would tell them "it's happening," the first thing He says is, "See to it that no one misleads you. For many will come in My name, saying, 'I am the Christ,' and they will mislead many people…For false christs and false prophets will arise and will provide great signs and wonders, so as to mislead, if possible, even the elect" (Matthew 24:3,24).

This is the final precursor prophecy leading to Antichrist. Today, we can detect and discern the spirit of Antichrist permeating our culture and even the church, as self-proclaimed prophets, messiahs, and spiritual gurus lead the masses away from the true Christ. Secularism, godless science, atheist philosophy, and higher education with a unified voice deny Jesus' deity. In addition, many churches and denominations have strayed from the truth Jesus taught in His Word and, by doing so, embrace the spirit of the Antichrist. Only those whose minds are biblically informed can test and discern this spirit so that it can be revealed and rejected (1 John 4:1).

#9 Is Antichrist Alive Today?

One of the distractions concerning this sensitive subject is the seemingly irresistible temptation to try to identify who Antichrist is or *might* be. We've already seen how this is not only a fruitless practice but also a very unbiblical one as Antichrist's identity cannot be known until after the "restrainer" (the Holy Spirit's influence of holding back great evil through the church) is removed at the rapture.

But even though we cannot now know his identity, we can know something of his *reality*. The apostle John doesn't instruct us to look for him, but he does prophetically warn us "antichrist is coming" (1 John 2:18). And there are several strong indicators pointing to the likelihood that Antichrist may very well be alive at this moment.

First, the rapture can happen at any time. We covered the doctrine of imminence in chapter 4, "The Rapture." When the rapture occurs, Antichrist must be alive, an adult, and ready to step into the chaotic void.

Second, zero prophecies remain unfulfilled prior to the rapture taking place. You could argue that Israel becoming a nation again is what's required in order for the rapture to take place. But theoretically that *could* have happened in the months following the rapture. However, in reality, Israel did become a nation on May 14, 1948. Since then, and especially in recent years, we've seen the preformation and foundation of some of Revelation's prophecies begin to materialize. This only further strengthens the argument that the rapture is very near.

Because of this proximity to coming fulfilled prophecy, Satan must have a potential Antichrist candidate ready to be catapulted into the forefront of history to lead the world into peace and safety. Presumably, the devil has had a potential Antichrist ready in every generation. Remember, he is not privy to God's prophetic timetable or precisely when the rapture will occur. However, in order to gain the respect of nations and to lead the world, this man must have accumulated some degree of political clout, even if in the shadows. And someone in their teens or twenties would not be able to accomplish that. Therefore, he will most likely be a bit older and more seasoned in the ways of worldly leadership.

> It is highly probable Antichrist is alive right now.

If the rapture occurred today, a man of some political stature and reasonable age would quickly step into the void and become Antichrist. But even if the blessed hope is 35 to 40 years from now, the Antichrist would still probably be alive right now, though at a relatively young age.

If we are not looking for Antichrist, what's the point of even knowing about him, *especially* if we are not going to be here on earth during his time? That's a very good question. We could apply the same question to 95 percent of Revelation since that's the percentage of future prophetic realities it covers. So why does God want us to know about what's going to happen in the future, particularly through this one individual? How does it directly impact us?

To begin with, *he is in the Bible*, so that makes him noteworthy. Second, there are more than 100 passages of Scripture that describe Antichrist's origin, character, kingdom, and destiny. Third, he is the most prominently prophesied end-times figure, second only to Jesus Christ Himself in terms of how much he's mentioned. Thirty-six times he is called the "beast" in Revelation. Fourth, he impacts and influences the entire planet during civilization's last days.

> He is the most-prominently foretold end-times figure, second only to Jesus Christ.

More specifically, knowing about Antichrist, his ways and evil reign, helps us recognize the spirit of Antichrist *right now*. It gives us insight into the "mystery of lawlessness" Paul spoke of in 2 Thessalonians 2:7. Through knowing what he is like and how he works, we can protect ourselves from that same devilish deception and subtle lies about God, salvation, truth, relationships, the afterlife, and even prophecy itself. We can also recognize current foreshadows of the global government he will bring together in that day.

By studying about Antichrist, we are given behind-the-scenes intelligence regarding not only Satan's plan for the world, but also God's plan for the ages as well. As Revelation 4 describes, there is an occupied throne standing in heaven. This tells us that God is still sovereign and in control, even over sin, Satan, and Antichrist. The story of Antichrist also teaches us much about God, including the truth that His justice and righteousness prevail in the end. Revelation 19 tells us that along with the false prophet, the Antichrist will be "thrown alive into the lake of fire, which burns with brimstone" (19:20). This is the place of eternal

punishment, from which there is no escape, no rest, and no reprieve. It's the same place of which John earlier wrote, describing its inhabitants' experience this way, "The smoke of their torment ascends forever and ever; they have no rest day and night" (Revelation 14:11). God wants us to look for the coming of Christ, but also to know about the future Antichrist and recognize his spirit working in our world today.

CHAPTER 8

THE PHYSICAL RETURN OF CHRIST

#1 What Are the Key Differences Between the First and Second Comings of Christ?

Everybody knows about the first coming of Christ as we rehearse it each year during the Christmas season. But what you might not know is that every time the first coming of Christ is mentioned in Scripture the second coming is mentioned *eight times*. Of the 333 prophecies concerning Jesus, 109 were fulfilled at His first coming, which leaves 224 remaining to be fulfilled.

But one of the biggest contrasts between Jesus' incarnation (Christmas) and appearing (second coming) are the purposes for each. When Christ came in the first century, He did so for three basic reasons:

1. To offer the messianic kingdom to the Jewish people, if they would only repent and receive it (Matthew 4:17,23; 9:35)

2. To reveal/explain God the Father (John 1:18)

3. To die as a substitute for our sins (Mark 10:45)

However, when He returns a second time, it will be for completely different reasons. This time, He is coming to bring wrath and retribution to His enemies (Revelation 19:11-21) and to establish His thousand-year millennial reign upon the earth (Revelation 20:1-6).

In the Old Testament, we see that Messiah is coming. In the New Testament, we see that He has come and that He is coming again.

COMPARING
THE 1ST & 2ND COMINGS

FIRST COMING	SECOND COMING
OFFERED KINGDOM	ESTABLISHES KINGDOM
REVEALED THE FATHER	REVEALS HIMSELF
DIED FOR SINNERS	PUNISHES SINNERS

FIRST COMING	SECOND COMING
Obscure, largely unnoticed	Every eye will see Him (Rev. 1:7)
Came as a suffering servant (Matt. 20:20-28; Mark 10:35-45; Phil. 2:5-8)	Returns as a conquering King (Rev. 19:11,15)
Came to bring redemption (Luke 19:10)	Returns to bring retribution (Rev. 19:11,15)
Offered His kingdom (Matt. 4:17)	Returns to establish His kingdom (Rev. 20:1-9)
Came in humility (Luke 2:16-20)	Returns in glory (Matt. 25:31)
Came to die (1 John 2:2)	Returns to reign (Luke 1:33; 2 Samuel 7:16)
His blood spilled by enemies (Isa. 53:1-10; John 19)	Returns to spill His enemies' blood (Rev. 19:13-15)
Came as a Lamb (John 1:29)	Returns as the Lion from Judah (Rev. 5:5; 12:5; 19:15)

Took on human flesh (John 1:14)	Returns in a glorified body (Rev. 1:12-16; 19:12)
Saved some of the Jews (Acts 2:37-41; Romans 1:16-17; 11:25-29)	Returns to save all Jews (Zechariah 13:8-9; Romans 1:16-17; 11:25-29)
His arrival in Jerusalem prophesied to the day (Dan. 9:24-26; Luke 19:27-44)	His return to Jerusalem unknown (Rev. 16:15)
His birthplace prophesied to be at Bethlehem (Micah 5:2; Matthew 2:1-6)	His return prophesied at Mount of Olives (Zechariah 12:9)

#2 What Are the Differences Between the Rapture and the Return of Christ?

We find an interesting word in the New Testament that describes the coming of the Lord. *Parousia* means "presence" or "arrival." In the secular world it was used to announce a king's arrival, and the New Testament writers seized on this word to describe the return of Jesus Christ. Of course, every word's specific meaning is always determined by the context in which it is used. And in the 24 times this word appears in the New Testament, 17 times it looks forward to the future return of Jesus. Among those 17 usages, 10 refer to the rapture, while 7 picture the second coming. It has been said that Christ's coming involves two phases: the rapture and the second coming. Nevertheless, these two events are distinct in many ways.

The primary purpose of the rapture is to rescue the bride of Christ (the church), delivering her from God's wrath unleashed during the tribulation (1 Thessalonians 1:10; 5:9; Revelation 3:10). The second coming has more to do with Israel and God's judgment upon the nations, culminating at Armageddon. If you believe the posttribulation view of the rapture (that it happens simultaneously with the second coming), then there is virtually no difference between the two appearances. However, if you believe the pre-trib rapture, the differences are unmistakable. For example,

THE RAPTURE...	THE SECOND COMING...
Is a sign-less event; imminent (Acts 1:6-7)[34]	Preceded by seven years of discernable signs and judgments (Rev. 6–19)
Jesus comes in the air (1 Thess. 4:16-17)	Jesus returns to the earth (Zech. 12:9; Rev. 19:11ff)
Jesus rescues us from wrath (1 Thess. 1:10; 5:9)	Jesus returns to deliver wrath (2 Thess. 2:8; Rev. 19:11)
Jesus rewards believers (1 Cor. 3:10-15; 4:5; 2 Cor. 5:10)	Jesus rewards unbelievers (Rev. 19:11-21)
Jesus returns *for* the church (1 Thess. 4:13-18)	Jesus returns *with* the church (Rev. 19:8, 14)
Jesus raises saints from the grave (1 Cor. 15:51-55; 1 Thess. 4:16)	Jesus puts the ungodly in the grave (Rev. 19:21)
Bride of Christ called to a wedding feast (John 14:3; Rev. 19:7-9)	Birds of the air called to a feast (Rev. 19:17-18)
Not prophesied in the Old Testament	Prophesied in both Old and New Testaments (Zech. 14:3-5; Matt. 24:29-31)
Occurs in an instant (1 Cor. 15:51-52; 1 Thess. 4:17)	Involves a battle campaign (Ps. 2:1-6; Isa. 24:1-7; 63:13; Rev. 16:12-16; 19-21)[35]
The tribulation begins afterward (Rev. 3:10)	The millennium begins afterward (Rev. 20:1-6)
The Savior of Calvary redeems (1 Cor. 15:55-56)	The Rider with cavalry judges (Rev. 19:11-16)
Only believers will see Him (1 Thess. 4:16-17; 1 John 3:2)	Every eye will see Him (Zech. 12:10; Rev. 1:7)

These two events will happen at least seven years apart. And it is important that we keep them separate because they serve two distinct purposes, one being exclusively for the church while the other has to do more with Israel and Gentile nations.

#3 Why Will Jesus Physically Return to Earth?

Revelation 19 details for us many of the specifics regarding Jesus' second coming. This monumental event occurs at the close of the seven-year period known as the tribulation. Many are familiar with the scenario of Christ showing up at the battle of Armageddon but may not know the actual reasons why He is returning. From Scripture, we can uncover at least seven primary motivations for what will prove to be the most dramatic moment in all of human history.

First, Jesus is returning because He said He would. He's going to fulfill the promise of His Word (Matthew 24:29-31; 25:31). The two angels at His ascension also prophesied that He would come back again, and as it turns out, to the exact same location (Acts 1:9-11). The prophet Zechariah also predicted this very same thing (Zechariah 14:4).

Second, Jesus will return to defeat His enemies (Revelation 19:19-21). For some, it's a disturbing concept to think about God having enemies. After all, He's supposed to love everyone, right? But Revelation makes it clear that "the kings of the earth and their armies [had] assembled to make war against Him who sat on the horse, and against His army" (Revelation 19:19). These armies will have been previously lured to Armageddon by three demons and for the express purpose of fighting God (Revelation 16:12-16). Unfortunately, for the millions of soldiers that will assemble upon that great battlefield, it will be no contest. In fact, it will be history's bloodiest and most brutal slaughter. Presumably, not a shot will be fired. Jesus will simply utter a word from His mouth and slay them all instantly on the spot (Revelation 19:15; Isaiah 11:4). And according to Revelation

14:17, He will be assisted by special angels in this battle (see also Matthew 13:39; 16:27). This is divine judgment, and another reason "it is a terrifying thing to fall into the hands of the living God" (Hebrews 10:31).

Third, Jesus will return to regather and restore Israel (Isaiah 11:11-12; 43:5-6; Jeremiah 30:10; 33:6-9; Ezekiel 36:22-38; 37:1-28; Romans 11:25-27). The seven-year time of tribulation is known in Scripture as the "time of Jacob's distress" (Jeremiah 30:7,10-11). Thus, His return will represent an end to Israel's suffering.

Fourth, He will at this time judge the Gentile nations (Matthew 25: 31-46). Those unbelievers who are alive at the time of Jesus' coming will face immediate, individual judgment from Him. This is also sometimes referred to as the "judgment of the sheep and the goats."

Fifth, Jesus will return to resurrect the Old Testament and tribulation saints (Revelation 20:4-6; Daniel 12:1-4). In order to enter the millennial kingdom, believers who have died before Christ came and during the tribulation will need their spirits clothed with glorified bodies like the ones given to the church at the rapture (1 Corinthians 15:51-54). It is at this time when the saints such as Job, Noah, Abraham, David, and John the Baptist will receive their glorified bodies (Job 19:25-27; Hosea 13:14).

Sixth, He is returning to bind Satan for a thousand years (Revelation 20:1-3). Amillennialists believe Satan is currently bound by Christ's finished work on the cross. But real life and Revelation 6–19 effectively refute this.

Seventh, Jesus returns to reign as King on the earth (Isaiah 9:6; Daniel 2:44; Matthew 19:28; Luke 1:32-33; Revelation 19:6).

#4 What Will the World See When Jesus Returns?

According to Scripture, Jesus' return will be both physical and visible. In fact, Revelation 1:7 claims that "every eye will see him" (see also Daniel 7:13; Matthew 24:29-30; 25:31-33). But how could this be?

Some have imagined this event being broadcast to the whole world. Others speculate social media will simultaneously explode with images of clouds parting and Jesus appearing. However, it may turn out to be much more supernatural in nature. Jesus may miraculously make Himself visible to every person, no matter where they are on the earth at that time. Perhaps this is a similar miracle to what God did in Revelation 14:6-7, where an angel flying at the height of our atmosphere preaches "with a loud voice" the eternal gospel "to every nation, tribe, language, and people" on the

earth. Somehow the whole world will hear him as people are graciously given one last chance to repent and turn to the true God. But when Jesus returns, there will be no time to repent.

So the whole world will finally look upon the most famous person in human history, a carpenter from Galilee. However, He will look nothing like they expect. Instead of being clothed as a humble Galilean, He will be robed in great splendor and glory. Consistent with the vision John received in Revelation 1, Jesus' eyes are a flame of fire and upon his head are many diadems (Revelation 19:12). He is riding a white horse (Revelation 19:11). Previously we saw another rider (Antichrist) on a white horse, coming "out conquering and to conquer" (Revelation 6:1-2).

Now the one who is "Faithful and True" and in righteousness "judges and wages war" is the one mounted upon a white horse. The Antichrist will witness this scene, further confirming his soon defeat and sealing his demise. The world will also see Him bursting through the clouds (Matthew 25:31; Revelation 19:14). Talk about making an entrance! But such a grand and global entrance is fitting for the "KING OF KINGS, AND LORD OF LORDS" (19:16).

Imagine the shock and terror that will grip every heart, captivating the attention of all those alive at that time. Armageddon also highlights how deceived the human heart can be, in that they join Satan, the Antichrist, and the false prophet in believing they can collectively defeat Almighty God. So every person on earth will view the Lord Jesus Christ riding earthward in brilliant glory. What a sight that is going to be!

#5 Who Will Come with Jesus When He Returns?

Jesus is not returning alone but instead is bringing an entire army with Him. This army has come from heaven (Revelation 19:14), and though we are not told the number, it is reasonable to imagine it being in the billions. Four groups accompany the Lord and make up this vast army here:

1. The bride of Christ (Revelation 19:8)
2. Believers who have died in the tribulation (Revelation 7:13-14)
3. Old Testament saints (Jude 14; Daniel 12:1-2)
4. Angels (Matthew 25:31)

The saints from the ages are riding these galloping white horses and following behind their conquering King and Captain of the Lord of Hosts (19:14-16).

It has been debated whether or not these are actual horses. But given the fact that there will be literal animals in the millennial kingdom (Isaiah

11:6-9; 56:7; Zechariah 14:6), and that there is nothing within the passage to suggest any symbolic interpretation, we take these horses to be literal and real, just as real as those riding upon them. The angels, however, likely do not ride horses but rather use their wings to travel. This means you will be riding behind Jesus on a white horse, witnessing firsthand His second coming and His defeat of His enemies at Armageddon.

What a front-row seat to history and to fulfilled prophecy! And you don't have to worry about not knowing how to ride a horse or about the severity of the judgment Jesus will render on that day. You will be in a glorified state without any of the limitations of humanity or the sin nature. You will see and understand justice, righteousness, and wrath the same way God does. In fact, you will actually rejoice in this day of vengeance (Romans 8:30; 1 Corinthians 15:53-54; 2 Corinthians 5:1-4; 1 John 3:1-2; Revelation 6:9-10).

#6 Where Exactly Will Jesus Touch Down When He Returns?

Perhaps no other apocalyptic word is more familiar to both Christian and secular minds than the word *Armageddon*. The mere mention of this word conjures up images of history's final battle and the end of the world. It's the war to end all wars, though according to the Bible, the battle actually ends before it even begins. But in reality, the so-called battle of Armageddon is actually a series of conflicts stretching from the mountain wilderness of Bozrah (about 80 miles south of Jerusalem) to the plain of Esdraelon, 50 miles to the north.

Scholars debate the exact chronology of Jesus' movements at His second coming. However, piecing together evidence from Scripture's prophecies, here's what we know will occur:

First, the Jewish remnant will call upon the Messiah for salvation and deliverance (Hosea 6:1-3; Joel 2:28-29; Zechariah 12:1–13:1; Matthew 23:37-39; Romans 10:13-14; 11:25-27). These Jews (representing a third of their population) have been hiding in the wilderness since the "abomination of desolation," which will occur at the midpoint of the tribulation (Daniel 9:27; Zechariah 13:8; Matthew 24:15-22).

Second, Jesus returns to the same spot from which He originally ascended (Zechariah 14:3-4; Acts 1:9-12). His touchdown there will be both dramatic and powerful. Dramatic, because He rides a white steed of victory and is armed for battle (Revelation 19:11). And powerful, in that when He lands upon the Mount of Olives, that mountain will split in half from east to west, causing it to move north and south. His authoritative landing will send reverberating aftershocks felt around the world, triggering the greatest earthquake in history. This earthquake will drastically alter the typography of the planet.

Mountains are leveled and islands will disappear into the oceans (Revelation 16:17-21). Jesus will then destroy Antichrist's forces who have seized Jerusalem (Zechariah 12:1-3). From there, He rides south to annihilate the Antichrist, the false prophet, and all their military might, as they had come there (Bozrah/Petra) to wipe out the Jews once and for all (Joel 3:12-13; Zechariah 14:12-15; Revelation 14:19-20).

Third, the conquering Christ, along with the armies of heaven

(Revelation 19:14), then travel to the valley of Megiddo (Armageddon), where He slays the armies of the nations using only the sword (word) of His mouth (Revelation 19:15-16,21).

It is not 100 percent clear whether Christ will first arrive at Bozrah to deliver the Jewish remnant there or whether His initial point of contact will be the Mount of Olives. But either way, these prophecies tell us that geography is a specific aspect of Jesus' return, one more indication that all these biblical predictions will be fulfilled literally and exactly as Scripture proclaims.

#7 What Will Jesus Do When He Returns?

The second coming of Jesus is taught in 23 of the 27 books in the New Testament, with over 300 references to this event. Jesus Himself spoke of His second coming about 20 times, one of which we find in Matthew 24:27-30:

> "For just as the lightning comes from the east and flashes as far as the west, so will the coming of the Son of Man be. Wherever the corpse is, there the vultures will gather. But immediately after the tribulation of those days the sun will be darkened, and the moon will not give its light, and the stars will fall from the sky, and the powers of the heavens will be shaken. And then the sign of the Son of Man will appear in the sky, and then all the tribes of the earth will mourn, and they will see the Son of Man coming on the clouds of the sky with power and great glory."

According to Revelation 19:11, there are two immediate purposes for Jesus' return: to judge and to wage war. And this is evidenced by the way Christ is described in the following verses:

> His eyes are a flame of fire, and on His head are many crowns; and He has a name written on Him which no one knows except

Himself. He is clothed with a robe dipped in blood, and His name is called The Word of God. And the armies which are in heaven, clothed in fine linen, white and clean, were following Him on white horses. From His mouth comes a sharp sword, so that with it He may strike down the nations, and He will rule them with a rod of iron; and He treads the wine press of the fierce wrath of God, the Almighty. And on His robe and on His thigh He has a name written, "KING OF KINGS, AND LORD OF LORDS" (Revelation 19:12-16).

This is the glorified Christ who is returning in great wrath to carry out vengeance upon a rebellious planet. For seven years, earth's inhabitants reveled in their sin, stubbornly refusing to repent of their wickedness (Revelation 9:20-21). On the contrary, they have grown angrier at God because of His judgments, shaking their fists, repeatedly cursing and blaspheming His name (Revelation 16:9,11,21). The collective heart of humanity is so depraved and eaten up with sin that they are now fully consumed by the spirit of Noah's wicked generation (Genesis 6:3).

But with sin also comes great deception, and the armies of the earth, lured by three powerful demons, rendezvous at Armageddon to fight God Himself (Revelation 16:12-16). In fact, Revelation 16:14 tells us this is *the* reason they have come together. They have declared war against Jesus' army (us) as well. But a manmade military force, even one energized by Satan, is no match for the infinite power inherent within Jesus Christ, who is the King of kings and Lord of lords.

The way John describes this scene is nothing short of terrifying. Jesus' eyes are a flame of fire (Revelation 19:12) and His robe is dipped in blood (19:13). This is possibly referring to Christ's slaughter of Antichrist's armies at Bozrah (Isaiah 34:6; Jeremiah 49:13-14; Micah 2:12). Out of His mouth comes a sharp (long) sword, which is merely His spoken word (19:15). During His earthly ministry, Christ often spoke words of comfort and healing. But here, His only words will be judgment and death. He "treads" upon them as one would grapes in a winepress, crushing and pulverizing them (19:15). His holy anger is described as the "fierce wrath of God, the Almighty" (19:15). This conquering war hero executes 100 percent of the millions gathered at Armageddon. An angel invites earth's remaining scavenger birds to come and feast upon the freshly slain corpses of "kings…commanders…and mighty men," including "both free and slaves, and small and the great" (19:17-18). And the birds fill their bellies with their flesh (19:21).

#8 What Does Jesus' Return Tell Us About Him?

The last book of the Bible is specifically called the "Revelation of Jesus Christ" and details the unveiling (revealing) of the prophecies "which must soon take place" (Revelation 1:1). It is a book *from* Jesus, *about* Jesus. And we learn dozens of truths regarding the nature and character of Christ, the Father, and the Spirit throughout. John's description of Jesus in chapter 1 alone is enough to radically impact our image and view of Him. But chapter 19 gives us great insight into Jesus as well. At His triumphant return, which is unquestionably the most climactic moment in human history, we discover several eye-opening truths about our Lord.

First, we see Him seated upon a white horse, and for a reason (19:11). It was customary for Roman generals to mount a white steed upon their return from a victorious battle campaign. Christ has traded in His humble donkey for a mighty war horse. This signifies Him as a conquering leader, and following behind Him are the "armies of heaven," which include the bride (Revelation 19:7-8), tribulation saints (Revelation 7:13-14), Old Testament believers (Jude 14; Daniel 12:1-2), and angels (Matthew 25:31).

Second, He is called here "Faithful and True" (Revelation 19:11). Revelation 1:5 calls Him "the faithful witness," and to the church at Laodicea, He is "the faithful and true Witness" (3:14). But faithful to what? To His Word. Jesus told His disciples in Matthew 24:27-31 that He would return one day "with power and great glory." Here in Revelation 19, Jesus makes good on that ancient promise. This is in perfect harmony with His trustworthy character, and tells us we can depend on Him to fulfill every other promise and prophecy He has made, including those we find in Revelation 6–19. After all, He is "the truth" (John 14:6).

Third, He is a righteous judge who wages war (Revelation 19:11). This is a typical description of Jesus. But His days as a suffering servant are over. In His first coming, He was judged and condemned to die by godless men (Acts 2:23; 3:13-15). But here, He returns as both judge and executioner

> **From suffering Savior to conquering King!**

upon a godless human race. This judgment is seen in His eyes ("a flame of fire," 19:12) and His mouth ("a sharp sword," 19:15). And with His word He will "strike down the nations," treading "the wine press of the fierce wrath of God, the Almighty" (19:15). The "many crowns" upon His head (19:12) speak of His regal authority to act in this way, and likely symbolize the seizing of power and authority of Antichrist's kings, as well as the beast's own crown, worn when he symbolically rode a white horse, "conquering and to conquer" at the tribulation's beginning (6:2). This is one reason Jesus is here called the "KING OF KINGS, AND LORD OF LORDS" (19:16). His sovereignty over all things is seen in the fact that not one shot at Christ or His armies is recorded in this passage. Instead, Jesus merely speaks the word, and in an instant, the enemy armies are all annihilated at Armageddon (Revelation 1:16; 14:20; 19:15,21; Isaiah 11:4; 63:1-4).

#9 What Will Happen After Jesus Defeats His Enemies?

After Jesus slays His enemies at Armageddon, all the birds of the earth are invited to come feast on their corpses (Revelation 19:17-19). The Antichrist and the false prophet are "seized" and thrown into the lake of fire (19:20). We're not told whether Christ or an angel lays hold of these two men. They are not given the opportunity to die, but are thrown alive into the dreaded lake of fire, becoming the first eternal residents of this awful place, where they are "tormented day and night forever and ever" (20:10).

The conquering Christ then turns His attention toward Antichrist's global army, mercilessly slaughtering them with the sword that comes from His mouth (19:21). What a horrendous scene of death that is simultaneously gory and glorious. This should send a wave of reverence reverberating through our souls as we contemplate the unrelenting wrath of the Lamb. It indeed is a terrifying thing to fall into the hands of the living God (Hebrews 10:31). Today, our generation is marked by the fact that "there is no fear of God before their eyes" (Psalm 36:1; Romans 3:18). And in the tribulation (and leading up to it), this pandemic of hardened hearts will exponentially increase as humanity repeatedly refuses to repent and consistently hates, curses, and blasphemes God and His Son (Romans 1:28-32; 2 Timothy 3:1-5; Revelation 9:20-21; 16:10-11,21). Here they had assembled to "make war" against Jesus Christ. Little did they realize that He had come to make war with *them*!

What follows this is a fascinating 75-day transitional period between the end of the tribulation and the inauguration of the millennial kingdom (Daniel 12:11-12).

Daniel gives us three lengths of time: 1,260 days (9:27), 1,290 days (12:11), and 1,335 days (12:12). Remember, the great tribulation lasts for 1,260 days (three-and-a-half years). And yet Daniel writes, "Blessed is the one who is patient and attains to the 1,335 days!" (12:12). If we take 1,335 and subtract 1,260, we're left with 75. So what is the purpose of the extra 30 and 45 days? And what will take place during this time?

This is similar to the period of time between when a president is elected (November) and when he is sworn in and takes office (January). Several important events will occur during this time.

First, the image of Antichrist in the rebuilt Jewish temple (abomination of desolation) will be taken down and removed 30 days after Jesus' return (Daniel 12:11). Daniel states this temple abomination will remain for 1,290 days (30 days longer than the final three-and-a-half years of the tribulation, which is 1,260 days in length). Within that 30-day period, the temple will be demolished and rebuilt for the millennial kingdom, as the tribulation temple may be irreparably damaged during the battles in Jerusalem or the impact of

Jesus' return on the Mount of Olives (Isaiah 2:2-4; Ezekiel 40–48; Haggai 2:6-9; Zechariah 6:9-15).

Second, Jesus judges Israel. During the 30-day period, remaining Israel is gathered together and judged as well (Ezekiel 20:33-38; Matthew 24:31; 25:1-30). They too will enter the kingdom in their earthly bodies.

Third, Jesus judges Gentile nations. This is the "sheep and the goats" judgment (Matthew 25:31-46). The place of judgment may be the now split halves of the Mount of Olives (Joel 3:2). Jesus will judge those living Gentiles whose faith in God is evidenced by their treatment of tribulation Jews (Jesus' "brothers or sisters," Matthew 25:40). Those without faith are sent to "the eternal fire" (v. 41), while those on His right "go away…into eternal life" (v. 46). These believers are not yet given glorified bodies but will enter the millennial kingdom in their mortal state and eventually die (Isaiah 65:20; Revelation 20:5).

Fourth, Satan is bound and thrown into the abyss (Revelation 20:1-3).

Fifth, God renovates a ravaged planet, preparing it for suitable kingdom habitation during the 45 remaining days, cleansing the land from the dead at Armageddon and other catastrophes. This time may also be used by Jesus to set up His government and assign kingdom responsibilities for us (Isaiah 65:17-21; Daniel 12:13).

Sixth, the original land borders promised to Israel (from Egypt to the Euphrates) will be established (Genesis 15:18).

Seventh, the celebration of the marriage supper of the Lamb will begin (Revelation 19:7-9). This will be a party like none other!

Whatever else happens during this time, we can be assured that it will involve great joy and celebration, as Christ has returned and is about to reign!

#10 Why Will Satan Be Chained Instead of Eternally Punished at the End of the Tribulation Period?

Among the most perplexing questions people ask are these: Why does God allow evil to exist, and why does He allow it to continue for so long? If the Antichrist and the false prophet are cast into the lake of fire, and Satan's wicked strategies have come to an end, why chain him up? Why not simply throw him into the lake of fire and be done with it? Knowing that Satan is like a lion with an insatiable appetite for evil, wouldn't it make more sense to send him on to his eternal punishment?

While we will address these questions more specifically in chapter 9, "The Literal Kingdom", let's look at what Scripture says is going to happen.

> Then I saw an angel coming down from heaven, holding the key of the abyss and a great chain in his hand. And he took hold of the dragon, the serpent of old, who is the devil and Satan, and bound him for a thousand years; and he threw him into the abyss, and shut it and sealed it over him, so that he would not deceive the nations any longer, until the thousand years were completed; after these things he must be released for a short time (Revelation 20:1-3).

THE ABYSS

SATAN

The Greek word translated "bound" here means to "tie up" or "put in chains." And notice that God Himself doesn't bind the dragon but rather sends an angel to perform this duty. This tells us that Satan is not the strongest of all the angels, but that he can be subdued by other angelic beings (cf. Revelation 12:7-9). The angel grabs the dragon, subdues him, puts him in chains, and throws him into the bottomless pit. The Greek word translated "chain" here is used elsewhere in Scripture to refer to literal chains (Mark 5:3-4; Acts 12:7; 28:20; 2 Timothy 1:16). As we have seen earlier, this abyss is the abode of demons, particularly ones who are in prison.

One would think that putting Satan in a bottomless pit and sealing the door over it would be sufficient to keep him locked away. But he is also wrapped in a great chain, indicating that even within the abode of demons, his power, influence, and activity are greatly restricted, rendering him impotent.

God obviously has a divine purpose for detaining Satan here instead of destroying him. One purpose is that He is not finished using him to display His righteousness and glory, as we will see at the close of the millennium. And because God is not finished with him, He must keep him from being active while Jesus judges the nations, prepares the earth, and sets up the government for His earthly kingdom. Then, once this 75-day transition from the tribulation to the kingdom is done, Satan will further need to be bound while we all enjoy the beauty, righteousness, and celebration of being in a world where Jesus alone rules supremely as King.

Satan is not currently bound. Rather, he is alive and well and masterminding evil on earth and in the spiritual realms (Ephesians 2:1-2). Some Christian traditions today believe in what is known as "binding Satan" through prayer or through some sort of declaration. However, this practice is nowhere mentioned or taught in Scripture. Christians also do not possess the power to bind Satan through some sort of word of faith declaration. If that were true, then the hundreds of millions of Christians across the world could simply keep him bound with their words. However, we *are* told that we can "resist the devil, and he will flee from you" (James 4:7). Of course, as he did with our Lord, he departs only to return at another "opportune time" (Luke 4:13).

CHAPTER 9

THE LITERAL KINGDOM

#1 Is the Kingdom of God Already Here?

God's kingdom is a prevalent theme throughout Scripture. King David prayed, "Yours, LORD, is the greatness, the power, the glory, the victory, and the majesty, indeed everything that is in the heavens and on the earth; Yours is the dominion, LORD, and You exalt Yourself as head over all" (1 Chronicles 29:11).

He repeated this theme in the Psalms:

- "The LORD is King forever and ever" (Psalm 10:16).
- "The LORD reigns...Your throne is established from of old" (Psalm 93:1,2).
- "Say among the nations, 'The LORD reigns'" (Psalm 96:10).

However, if all this is true, then why does the world seem to be so out of control? Why so much chaos, catastrophe, and suffering? If God is King and this is His kingdom, then why does it feel like no one is on the throne?

Some Christian traditions and denominations believe God's kingdom is already here. Both John the Baptist and Jesus heralded, "Repent, for the kingdom of heaven is at hand" (Matthew 3:2; 4:17). And Jesus later proclaimed, "The kingdom of God is in your midst" (Luke 17:21). But

Scripture also says that believers will one day "reign upon the earth" with Christ (Revelation 3:21; 5:10; 20:4-6; 22:5).

So, which is it? Is the kingdom here now? Or is it yet to come? The answer is yes to both questions!

When the Bible speaks of God's kingdom, it's referring to His sovereignty or rule over all there is. From eternity past, God has always reigned supremely. And He ruled in heaven before the creation of the universe.

But the Lord's rightful rule over His creation was challenged in the Garden of Eden and during the sin-soaked days of Noah. Each time, God responded with both judgment and mercy (Genesis 3; 6–9.) Eventually, He reestablished His kingdom program through a special arrangement with the Jewish nation (Israel). This relationship was facilitated through promise agreements (or covenants) He made with Abraham (Genesis 12:1-3; 15:1-21), and David (2 Samuel 7:8-16).

In time, He sent His Son to be their Messiah. Jesus came, presenting Himself to the Jewish nation as their righteous King. This is why both He and John the Baptist spoke of God's kingdom as being "near" and "in your midst." However, instead of embracing God's Son as their prophesied king, Israel rejected Him and His offer of the kingdom (Matthew 12:25-28; 21:42-44; John 1:11).

JESUS   RELIGIOUS LEADERS

As a result, the long-awaited fulfillment of God's promised kingdom would have to be postponed until a later time. In fact, the entire church age and future tribulation period will pass before future aspects of God's kingdom will be realized for Israel (Isaiah 60; Romans 11:25-27). This is the kingdom you're praying for in the "Lord's Prayer."

So, if that's the future establishment of His future reign, is there a sense in which His kingdom is here and now? And how do we participate in it?

Though Satan is called the "god of this world," God still rules supreme over the earth, nations, and universe (Psalm 47:8; 93; Isaiah 40:12-26; 2 Corinthians 4:3-4). At Jesus' return, He will officially end Satan's dominion. Second, God also reigns as King in believers' hearts and in the church, over which He is the head (Matthew 6:33; Acts 28:30-31; 2 Corinthians 5:20; Colossians 1:18; 1 Peter 3:15). While on earth, we Christians live under the rule (kingdom) of Christ, who has rescued us from the dominion (kingdom) of darkness (Colossians 1:13-14). Daily recognizing Him as our King helps us lead lives worthy of His kingdom (1 Thessalonians 2:13-14).

THE KINGDOM ...IS NOW. ...HAS ALWAYS BEEN. ...IS COMING.

So, whether in the past with Israel, in the present through the church, or in the future through Christ's reign and reestablished Davidic throne, God's kingdom manifests itself in various forms and expressions. And yet, throughout all of it, He remains the unrivalled sovereign over the universe. Right here. Right now.

#2 Why Will There Be a Millennial Kingdom?

Following Jesus' second coming, God could have moved us right into heaven and eternity. So why does He plan on establishing an earthly kingdom? What's the point of it? There are several purposes, actually, and many of them have to do with God keeping His promises to Israel. But first, the main reason there will be a millennial kingdom is to give Jesus what is rightfully His—preeminence and dominion over all (Psalm 2:7-8; Colossians 1:15-18; Hebrews 1:1-2).

Second, during the millennial kingdom, God will fulfill the totality of His promise to Abraham regarding blessing of his seed and the land originally given to Israel (Genesis 12:2-3; 15:18-21). Their possession was meant to stretch from the Nile River in Egypt to the Euphrates River (Genesis 15:18), and from Mount Hor to Hazar-enan (Numbers 34:7-9). And what is so significant about this promise? Genesis 13:14-15 provides the answer for us:

> The LORD said to Abram, after Lot had separated from him, "Now raise your eyes and look from the place where you are, northward and southward, and eastward and westward; for all the land which you see *I will give it to you and to your descendants forever*."[36]

God's agreement with Abraham and his descendants is to be an "everlasting covenant," deeding to him "all the land of Canaan, as an everlasting possession; and I will be their God" (Genesis 17:7-8). This establishes not only a perpetual covenant but also an unconditional one as well. God Himself guarantees this possession for Abraham's covenant descendants, which is Israel.

We know from the historical record that Israel has never possessed these biblical boundaries, not under Joshua's initial conquest or even during Solomon's expansive reign (1 Kings 4:21-24). Therefore, if they've never possessed these land boundaries, then it must be still a future prophetic reality, finding its fulfillment in a future kingdom.

Third, God promised that the Messiah would reign on David's throne forever, and of His government there will be no end (2 Samuel 7:10-17; 1 Chronicles 17:11-14; 2 Chronicles 6:14-17; Isaiah 9:6-7; 11:1). Finally, the promise of the new covenant (for Israel to seek God from her heart) will also see its fulfillment in the millennial kingdom (Psalm 72:8; Jeremiah 31:31-34; 32:35-40; Ezekiel 11:18-20; 16:60-63; 37:24-28; Daniel 7:13-14; Zechariah 9:10; Romans 11:25-29).

In Matthew 4:8-10 and Luke 4:5-8, Satan offered Jesus all the kingdoms of the world, including the glory that comes with them. Christ refused this offer because He knew it was foolish to worship anyone other than the true God (Deuteronomy 6:13-15). But He also knew that one day the kingdoms of this world would legitimately belong to Him (Revelation 11:15). The millennial kingdom will also see God rewarding His people from all ages for their faithful service to Him. It is during this kingdom establishment when creation will be restored as well. But more about these purposes in questions 6–8 below.

#3 Who Will Inhabit the Millennial Kingdom?

Christ's kingdom will be abundantly populated and as diverse as humanity itself. It will contain representatives "from every tribe, language, people, and nation" (Revelation 5:9-10; 7:9). This is how great the grace of God is. In Matthew 7:13-14, Jesus contrasts the broad way with the narrow way, declaring that only a "few" will ultimately find it. And while, compared to the rest of humanity's billions, true believers will be a minority, that "few" is still much greater than we imagine. Among those who will inhabit this thousand-year kingdom are:

Old Testament saints. They are resurrected and given glorified bodies in order to enter the millennial kingdom (Isaiah 26:19; Daniel 12:2). This is the same kingdom that was promised to them in the Old Testament and subsequently offered to them at Jesus' first coming (Matthew 3:1-2; 4:17).

Tribulation saints (Jews and Gentiles). This group is made up of those who died or were martyred during that time. They are also resurrected to reign with Christ in His thousand-year kingdom (Revelation 20:4).

Tribulation saints (Jews and Gentiles) who are alive at the time of the second coming (Zechariah 12:10; Matthew 25:31-46). These will be ushered into the kingdom, where their life spans will apparently be greatly lengthened in this new environment (Isaiah 34:24; Ezekiel 34:25-28; Zechariah

14:10-11). These tribulation-era Christians who transition into the millennial kingdom will not yet have glorified bodies because they have neither died nor been raptured. Including both Jews and Gentiles, they will be able to marry and reproduce, unlike those who have been granted heavenly bodies (Jeremiah 30:20; Ezekiel 47:21-23; Zechariah 10:8; Matthew 22:30).

The bride of Christ (the church). This consists of those who are saved from the time of the birth of the church (Acts 2) to the rapture (John 14:1-3; 1 Thessalonians 4:13-18). Having been previously delivered from the "wrath to come" (tribulation—Revelation 6–18), the church will return from heaven with Jesus at His second coming, riding behind Him on white horses (Revelation 19:8,14).

> **CHRIST'S KINGDOM will contain representatives from every tribe and tongue and people and nation (Revelation 5:10; 7:9).**

Adam, Abraham, David, Solomon, Elijah and the prophets, John the Baptist, Mary, the apostles, Paul, and all those who trusted in Jesus down through the centuries will be there. You may wonder whether we will know one another in that day, and the answer is yes! We will all be united in Him and recognize each other (Matthew 17:1-4).

#4 Will There Be Sin in the Millennial Kingdom?

This question, along with number 10 at the end of this chapter, may be the most perplexing of the 100 questions we address in this book. And the explanation may still not relieve the tension we feel. Even so, the short answer is that sin *will* exist in the millennial kingdom. But two additional questions immediately arise from this reality: How could sin be there? And why would Jesus ever allow it?

The *how* here is much easier to address than the *why*. Remember in question #3, we learned that tribulation Christians alive at the time of Christ's second coming will transition straight into the millennium. In terms of their bodies and relationship with God, they are very similar to what we are now—saved but still in a mortal body. Because of this, they are susceptible to the desires of the sin nature that still resides within them (Jeremiah 17:9; Romans 7:18; Galatians 5:16-21). Like us, they do not *have* to sin, but inevitably they will.

However, three things we should keep in mind here:

1. Their outward behavior in the millennial kingdom will probably be somewhat (but not completely) restricted by the sinless redeemed with whom they fellowship, a sort of "godly kingdom peer pressure."

2. But sinful behavior will also be curbed by the presence of Christ on His throne (Ezekiel 37:27-28; Zechariah 2:10-13). It is difficult to think of blatantly sinning when you're in the vicinity of Jesus, though it will undoubtedly happen. In fact, we will all be perpetually "in His presence," as Jerusalem will be referred to as *Yahweh-shammah* ("the LORD is there"—Ezekiel 48:35).

3. Christ's reign of righteousness will ensure that sin and disobedience are swiftly addressed with divine discipline and justice (Isaiah 9:7; 11:5; 32:16; 42:1-4; 65:21-23).

As to why Jesus would allow this in His kingdom, Scripture does not give us a definitive answer. But we do learn two very important truths from this reality. First, even in a perfect environment, and with Jesus present, humans

NATURAL BODY

GLORIFIED BODY

are still capable of sin. This highlights the depth of our inherent depravity and explains why Jeremiah wrote, "Who can understand [the heart]?" (Jeremiah 17:9). Second, it also demonstrates how susceptible we are to Satan's deceptions, even after living in an alternative kingdom full of love and righteousness.

#5 What Will Worship Be Like in the Millennial Kingdom?

One of the aspects of Jesus' thousand-year reign will be uninhibited worship and adoration (Isaiah 45:23; 52:1,7-10; 66:18-23; Zephaniah 3:9-10; Zechariah 13:2; 14:16; Malachi 1:11). But Scripture indicates our worship will be centralized in Jerusalem, in a rebuilt temple (Ezekiel 40:1-46). There will be animal sacrifices as well (Isaiah 56:6-7; 60:7; Ezekiel 43:18-27; Zechariah 14:16-21). But why? Why a temple and why animal sacrifices...*again*? Isn't that part of the old covenant and the Old Testament sacrificial system Christ did away with at the cross? What about Hebrews 9:11-12?

> But when Christ appeared as a high priest of the good things having come, He entered through the greater and more perfect tabernacle, not made by hands, that is, not of this creation; and not through the blood of goats and calves, but through His own blood, He entered the holy place once for all, having obtained eternal redemption.

And doesn't Hebrews 10:4 state, "It is impossible for the blood of bulls and goats to take away sins"? Absolutely. So why a temple and why sacrifices?

This fourth temple and its sacrifices are in no way either a reinstatement of the Mosaic law or a replacement for the precious, sufficient, and eternal sacrifice Christ made for us "once for all time" (Hebrews 7:27). Instead, it is possible the sacrifices serve as a reminder and a symbolic memorial to the death of Christ for us, much like the Lord's Supper does for us today. Purely symbolic. *Not* salvific.

However, Ezekiel states that these sacrifices *are* for "atonement." But this word used in Ezekiel 40–48 refers to "ceremonial purification or consecration of the temple or altar."[37]

Mark Hitchcock comments, "A better explanation is that these sacrifices serve as ritual purification. During the millennium, a holy God will be dwelling on earth in the midst of sinful people...living in natural, unglorified bodies. These sacrifices prevent these worshipers from defiling God's holy temple when they come to worship him. It's a matter of ritual purification."[38]

Our worship in the millennial kingdom will be unhindered and different from what we have enjoyed for seven short years in heaven (during the tribulation). As Isaiah records, "'All mankind will come to bow down before me,' says the LORD" (Isaiah 66:23). Our fellowship with all the saints will be visible, tangible, and a multisensory experience as we enter His temple and enjoy His kingdom. And our praise will fill the whole earth.

#6 What Will Our Roles Be in the Millennial Kingdom?

Scripture gives us multiple clues about our privileges, responsibilities, and relationship with God during this time. First, we will *reign* with Christ. Daniel, writing about the end of days, prophesied,

> "'But the saints of the Highest One will receive the kingdom
> and take possession of the kingdom forever, for all ages to come.'
> "...until the Ancient of Days came and judgment was passed

in favor of the saints of the Highest One, and the time arrived when the saints took possession of the kingdom.

"'Then the sovereignty, the dominion, and the greatness of all the kingdoms under the whole heaven will be given to the people of the saints of the Highest One; His kingdom will be an everlasting kingdom, and all the empires will serve and obey Him'" (Daniel 7:18,22,27).

John was also given information about our future millennial reign: "Then I saw thrones, and they sat on them, and judgment was given to them...Blessed and holy is the one who has a part in the first resurrection; over these the second death has no power, but they will be priests of God and of Christ, and will reign with Him for a thousand years" (Revelation 20:4,6).

This co-rulership with Jesus may be tough to wrap our heads around. Nevertheless, Scripture states that it includes:

Judging angels (1 Corinthians 6:1-3). Because God Himself will judge the fallen angels (2 Peter 2:4; Jude 6), this must then refer to godly angels. The word *judge* here likely refers to ruling or governing over them. Angels already have a role in serving believers (Hebrews 1:14), so apparently this angelic responsibility will continue on into the kingdom, where they will continue to minister to us.

Ruling over cities (Luke 19:11-26) *and even nations* (Revelation 2:26-28). According to Scripture, the degree of our rulership/governance is determined by our obedience, faithfulness, and overcoming in this present life. Therefore, our current faithfulness greatly influences our future rewards.

#7 How Will the Environment of the World Change in the Millennial Kingdom?

The landscape of the earth will radically change during Revelation's seven-year tribulation. Due to catastrophic disasters and cosmic disturbances, the terrain will be altered, rendering it virtually uninhabitable. Imagine the long-term effects of the following occurrences: global war (Revelation 6:3-4); billions of deaths (Revelation 6:8; 9:18); massive, repeated earthquakes (Revelation 6:12-14; 8:5; 16:18-19); rivers and oceans polluted (Revelation 8:8; 16:4); devastation from meteors and asteroids (Revelation 6:13; 8:10); one-third of the trees burned up and all the green grass burned (Revelation 8:7); widespread pollution from war, potentially a nuclear fallout (Revelation 6:4,8); and numerous volcanic eruptions due to earthquakes (Revelation 6:12).

Combined, all these will undoubtedly make our planet a very undesirable place to live. With the current obsession and global narrative associated with climate change, ironically it turns out that God Himself will be responsible for dramatically transforming the terrain, changing the atmosphere, and threatening the sustainability of our planet. It will be a worst-nightmare scenario for those who devoted their energies, ideologies, and finances to this climate theory. Yes, climate change *is* coming…on steroids! It is inevitable and will be initiated by the Creator.

However, fortunately God's plan also includes remaking the topography and renewing the atmosphere in order to prepare a more suitable place for us during the millennium. From Scripture, we learn that Jerusalem will be the capital of the world and of Christ's kingdom (Isaiah 2:3). There

> **Deserts will bloom with flowers, and instead of famine and drought, there will be plenty of rain and food** (Isaiah 30:23-24; 35:1-7).

will be no more war to ravage mankind or the earth (Isaiah 2:4). Deserts will bloom with flowers, and instead of famine and drought, there will be plenty of rain and food (Isaiah 30:23-24; 35:1-7). As earlier mentioned, the Lord will use the 75-day interval between the second coming and the inauguration of the kingdom to essentially restore the earth to its original state at creation. Genesis 1:31 records that at the close of the sixth day of creation, everything was "very good." Eden was paradise, and humanity was privileged to live in a world that was ecologically and theologically perfect. That day is coming again!

God will also restore the mountains that have been leveled, while simultaneously turning the area all around Jerusalem into a vast plain, with the city itself rising above it like a jewel (Micah 4:1; Zechariah 14:9-10; Revelation 16:20). Even now, our entire planet groans for redemption and restoration to its original state, as sin's entrance into the world adversely affected all of creation (Genesis 3:17-19; Romans 8:20-22). But in that day, God will restore all things to the original beauty and glory that Adam and Eve once enjoyed.

I CAN'T WAIT!

#8 How Will Animals Change in the Millennial Kingdom?

Oddly enough, one of the most frequent questions we get is whether our pets will be in heaven. Scripture does not directly address the eternal state of domestic animals. But this we do know with certainty. Unlike humans, animals are not made in the image of God (Genesis 1:26-27). Though they are pleasant and personal to us, and we may care deeply for them, nevertheless they do not possess souls, and Christ did not purchase eternal life for them on the cross. There is also nothing in the Bible regarding the resurrection of animals, them being glorified, or being given any kind of new heavenly bodies. Therefore, there is insufficient evidence to suggest that billions of pets throughout history (dogs, cats, goldfish, hamsters, birds, horses, snakes) will be waiting for their owners in the millennial kingdom.

That being true, the good news is that the Bible *does* tell us there will be animals in Christ's future kingdom. These will be akin to those originally created by God and named by Adam in the Garden of Eden (Genesis 1:20-25; 2:19-20). But what will these animals be like? To begin, they will harbor no effects of sin within them. When Adam fell, sin flowed forth, polluting and impacting all living things (Genesis 3:14). This is why animals kill one another and can be hostile to humans. However, in the millennium, the curse on the animal kingdom will be reversed. Peace and harmony will be brought back into prominence, and as Isaiah prophesied,

> And the wolf will dwell with the lamb,
> And the leopard will lie down with the young goat,
> And the calf and the young lion and the fattened steer will be
> together;
> And a little boy will lead them.
> Also the cow and the bear will graze,
> Their young will lie down together,
> And the lion will eat straw like the ox.

The nursing child will play by the hole of the cobra,
And the weaned child will put his hand on the viper's den.
(Isaiah 11:6-8)

We will not fear any animal for not one "vicious animal" will dwell on earth (Isaiah 35:9; 65:25). Mankind was originally made to be a coregent with God, as the Lord gave humans dominion over the entire animal kingdom, including birds, beasts, and all sea creatures (Genesis 1:26-28; Psalm 8:3-8). The millennial kingdom will see the restoration of that dominion and privilege for us. We may even continue to enjoy the white horse provided for us at the second coming (Revelation 19:14).

#9 What Will the Government Be Like in the Millennial Kingdom?

None of us has ever lived under a perfect government. But under Jesus' administration, that's going to change. *First*, and most importantly, Christ will be King. Consequently, the spirit, character, and operation of this government will reflect His divine nature. Gone forever are corrupt politicians, partisan policies, and nefarious dealings. In their place will be integrity, justice, and honor. All judgments and decisions in the kingdom are guided by God's nature and marked by unparalleled wisdom, righteousness, and fairness. And in place of war, there will be peace (Psalm 72; Isaiah 9:6-7; 11:1-5). The prophet Isaiah writes,

> And they will beat their swords into plowshares, and their spears into pruning knives.

Nation will not lift up a sword against nation,
And never again will they learn war.
(Isaiah 2:4)

Second, Christ's kingdom will encompass the whole earth (Psalm 2:6-9; Daniel 7:14), with its headquarters in Jerusalem (Isaiah 2:2-4; Ezekiel 48:30-35; Micah 4:1,6-8; Zechariah 8:1-3).[39]

Third, Jesus' government will last forever (Isaiah 9:7; Daniel 7:14,27).

Fourth, part of living under His rule will be the enjoyment of spiritual blessings and benefits never before experienced. And *everyone* will know the Lord in that day (Isaiah 11:9). The prophet Jeremiah describes it this way: "I will put My law within them and write it on their heart; and I will be their God, and they shall be My people. They will not teach again, each one his neighbor and each one his brother, saying, 'Know the LORD,' for they will all know Me, from the least of them to the greatest of them," declares the LORD" (Jeremiah 31:33-34).

Fifth, there will also be no knowledge gap between believers, and every glorified saint will have graduated into full spiritual maturity (Romans 8:29-30). All of our questions will be answered in the kingdom, as we will have perpetual access to the Source of knowledge and wisdom. All our doubts are a thing of the past. And the mysteries that once perplexed us are finally revealed (Deuteronomy 29:29; Daniel 2:28). We will possess the full "mind of Christ" (Isaiah 11:1-2,9; 54:13; 1 Corinthians 2:16; 13:12).

Sixth, all the saints will worship Him together in Jerusalem (Ezekiel 40–48; Isaiah 45:23; 52:1,7-10; 66:18-21; Zephaniah 3:9; Zechariah 13:2; 14:16; Malachi 1:11). There will also be a rebuilt temple (Isaiah 2:3; 60:13; Ezekiel 43:1-9,18-27; Joel 3:18; Haggai 2:7-9).[40]

Seventh, we will enjoy the firstfruits of eternal life in God's presence. We'll be filled with joy, peace, holiness, justice, righteousness, and health.[41] Many other glorious surprises await us in this millennial reign. Truly, it will be a foretaste of things to come in eternity, like heaven on earth!

#10 Why Will Satan Be Loosed at the End of the Millennial Kingdom?

After a thousand years of being chained and held inside the dark abyss (bottomless pit), Satan will be released (Revelation 20:1-3,7). In Revelation, this abyss always refers to a temporary prison for the worst of demons (9:1-2,11; see also Genesis 6:1-2; 1 Peter 3:19-20; Jude 6). It is a place most feared by the demonic host. And for a millennium, Satan resides there alone, stewing in hatred for Jesus Christ. Whenever he is defeated or punished, his anger and fury only become more intense (Revelation 12:7-9,12-13).

Released from the bottomless pit, Satan bolts with a final fury fueled by an inherent wickedness that cannot be adequately described with words. His hatred, combined with his desire to rule and deceive, motivates his one final strategy.

> When the thousand years are completed, Satan will be released from his prison, and will come out to deceive the nations which are at the four corners of the earth, Gog and Magog, to gather them together for the war; the number of them is like the sand of the seashore. And they came up on the broad plain of the earth and surrounded the camp of the saints and the beloved city, and fire came down from heaven and devoured them (Revelation 20:7-9).

So who are "Gog and Magog"? They are certainly not the "Gog and Magog war" of Ezekiel 38–39. That battle, though still future as well, describes a completely separate event, and takes place sometime between

Israel's national rebirth and her spiritual rebirth, during the "latter years" and "last days," when Israel is "living securely" and at peace in the land (Ezekiel 37–40; 38:8,14,16). And since there are no wars during the millennium, it must occur some other time, most likely in the early days of the tribulation, following Antichrist's peace treaty with Israel (Daniel 9:27).

The reference to "Gog" here in Revelation 20 would then describe a different person leading a satanic army. Under his command is a horde of humanity that has allowed themselves to be deceived by the devil. Remember, the saved coming out of the tribulation are still in their mortal bodies, and over the span of a thousand years, lots of children are born to these believers and to their children's children, and so on (Isaiah 65:20). This is the only way to explain how there could be unconverted masses during this time.

Some from this multitude refuse salvation, succumbing to the rebellion sold to them by Satan. Coming from all over the earth (Revelation 20:8), this army of darkness will surround Jerusalem, with intentions to annihilate her. But before they can launch an attack, fire descends from heaven, consuming them and leaving no trace of their presence behind.

And so Satan's final rebellion meets the same result as his previous ones, only with a much more severe and permanent punishment. The devil is cast into the lake of fire, joining the Antichrist and the false prophet, who have been there for a thousand years (Revelation 19:20). There they all will remain, "tormented day and night forever and ever" (Revelation 20:10).

But why would God release him in the first place? Why not just send him to the lake of fire straight from the abyss? We believe he is released

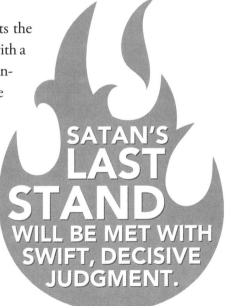

SATAN'S LAST STAND WILL BE MET WITH SWIFT, DECISIVE JUDGMENT.

to prove his unredeemable nature and to further demonstrate the inherent wickedness of the human heart (Jeremiah 17:9; Romans 3:10-12; 7:18). Very soon, the devil's former servants and fellow demons will be cast there as well (Matthew 25:41; 2 Peter 2:4; Jude 6). Satan is also released so that God may display before all that He has now dealt with sin and sinners for the last time. There will never again be any remnant of evil among God's beloved people.

CHAPTER 10

THE ETERNAL STATE

#1 Why Does the Bible Talk About a *First* and a *Second* Resurrection?

John writes in Revelation 20:4-6,

> Then I saw thrones, and they sat on them, and judgment was given to them. And I saw the souls of those who had been beheaded because of their testimony of Jesus and because of the word of God, and those who had not worshiped the beast or his image, and had not received the mark on their foreheads and on their hands; and they came to life and reigned with Christ for a thousand years. The rest of the dead did not come to life until the thousand years were completed. This is the first resurrection. Blessed and holy is the one who has a part in the first resurrection; over these the second death has no power, but they will be priests of God and of Christ, and will reign with Him for a thousand years.

These verses tell us about two separate resurrections, the first of which takes place just prior to the start of the millennial kingdom. The participants in this bodily resurrection are the martyrs of the tribulation. Having postponed their decision for Christ prior to the rapture, their subsequent salvation cost them dearly, including hunger, thirst, suffering under the tribulation's judgments, and ultimately, their heads (Revelation 7:16; 20:4).

It is also at this time that past saints are resurrected and endowed with glorified bodies (Luke 14:14; John 5:29; Acts 24:15). This is the "better resurrection" promised to all Old Testament saints (Hebrews 11:35). Everyone who placed trust in Yahweh, from Adam to Abraham to the very last one to believe prior to the church's birth (Acts 2), will be brought to life here. They are called "blessed," because the second death (eternal punishment) has no power over them, and because "they will be priests of God and of Christ, and will reign with Him for a thousand years" (Daniel 12:2; Revelation 20:6). This is the final transformation for them, completing the physical aspect of their salvation.

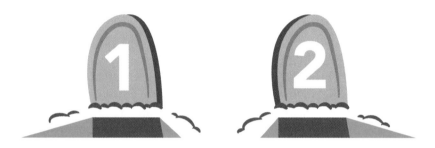

The second resurrection spoken of here takes place at the end of the millennial kingdom (Revelation 20:5). It is a resurrection to judgment and involves unbelievers from all ages.

#2 What Is the Great White Throne (or Final) Judgment?

Perhaps the most chilling of all scenes described in Scripture is found in Revelation 20:11-15. It is commonly known as the Great White Throne judgment. We read in verses 11-13,

> Then I saw a great white throne and Him who sat upon it, from whose presence earth and heaven fled, and no place was found

for them. And I saw the dead, the great and the small, standing before the throne, and books were opened; and another book was opened, which is the book of life; and the dead were judged from the things which were written in the books, according to their deeds. And the sea gave up the dead who were in it, and Death and Hades gave up the dead who were in them; and they were judged, each one of them according to their deeds.

While some are previously resurrected to life and glory, these here are resurrected out of hell for judgment at the close of the millennial kingdom (Revelation 20:5). The same word used for the resurrection of the righteous is also used to describe the resurrection of these condemned ones, signifying that they will be given some sort of *physical bodies* with which they will suffer God's wrath throughout eternity.

The judge sitting on this throne is the Lord Jesus Christ (John 5:22; Acts 10:42; Philippians 2:8-11). Imagine this scene: Gathered before Him is every unbeliever from all time (Revelation 20:12). Every participant in this judgment longs to run for safety, but they are unable (20:11). "Books" are opened, one containing a record of their evil deeds (20:12-13) and the other being the "book of life." Each person stands individually before Jesus the Judge. Every sinful thought, word, action, and motive is made known in heaven's high court (Jeremiah 17:10; Matthew 12:36-37; Romans 2:9,14-16). Every time a person ignored, dismissed, procrastinated, scoffed at, or rejected the truth of Jesus and the offer of salvation—all of this will be rehearsed for them. They are completely without defense or excuse.

There is no appeal process in this supreme court of heaven, and no defense attorney, since the one who would've defended them is now acting as their judge (1 John 2:1). They are all silent before God, as they have already spent time in hell contemplating their regret for rejecting Jesus Christ during their lifetime. This is Exhibit A.

Exhibit B is brought forth, which is the book of life. This book contains names recorded there before the foundation of the world (Luke 10:20; Ephesians 1:3-4; Revelation 3:5; 13:8; 20:12,15). If your name is not found there, you hear the most dreaded words ever to reach the human ear, "Depart from Me, you accursed people, into the eternal fire which has been prepared for the devil and his angels" (Matthew 25:41). "This is the second death, the lake of fire" (Revelation 20:14). Only by trusting in Christ and His work on the cross can a person be delivered from this terrifying great white throne judgment.

EXHIBIT A   EXHIBIT B

#3 What Is the Lake of Fire? Are There Degrees of Punishment in Hell and of Reward in Heaven?

Revelation first introduces the concept of a "lake of fire" in 19:20 when the Antichrist and the false prophet are cast there following Armageddon. Mentioned six times in Revelation, the lake of fire is another way to describe eternal hell. It was originally created for the devil and his angels who rebelled in heaven before man was created (Matthew 25:41). It is described as:

- Fire and *brimstone,* a sulphury burning rock, associated with God's wrath and judgment (Genesis 19:24; Deuteronomy

4:24; Luke 17:28-29; Hebrews 12:29; Revelation 14:10; 19:20; 21:8).

- Those cast into this massive, burning lake possess physical bodies that the fire torments, and yet somehow does not consume. And they are eternally imprisoned there with no chance of escape, pardon, or even a single second of relief (Mark 9:43-48; Revelation 14:10-11).

- It's a place of unimaginable torment (Luke 16:23-24; Revelation 14:10-11). Part of the agony in the lake of fire is the pain of God's infinite wrath, while the other is the "outer darkness" associated with it. There is no pain this side of eternity that remotely resembles it.

- There is no light there, as "God is Light, and in Him there is no darkness at all" (1 John 1:5). His light represents goodness and righteousness, neither of which is a part of the lake of fire experience (2 Thessalonians 1:6-10).

- Eternal hell is also a place where Jesus rules, not Satan (Revelation 14:10). Contrary to ancient myth and modern folklore, Satan and his demons do not torment those in hell. It's impossible, for at least two reasons: 1) God's wrath is what punishes, not Satan, and 2) the devil will be too preoccupied with being tormented himself!

- The lake of fire represents the greatest expression of God's righteous fury, being a place of "weeping and gnashing of teeth" (Matthew 13:41-42). Combine an omnipotent God with the anger of His wrath toward sin and you get a level of agony no words can possibly describe. We are simply told His wrath will be mixed in "full strength" (Revelation 14:10).

- It's a place producing "smoke" (Revelation 14:11). The continual burning of body and soul will result in a sulfurous smoke rising up before God (Isaiah 34:8-10).

- It lasts forever; it's constant and eternal (Matthew 18:8; 25:46; 2 Thessalonians 1:6-10; Revelation 14:11).

The lake of fire is incomprehensible. And every person on earth should be warned of its reality.

Another misconception about this eternal lake of fire is that everyone will suffer equally. However, this idea is not supported in Scripture. Revelation 20:11-13 twice states that each person's judgment will be "*according to* their deeds." This debunks the popular phrase so often used by Christians that "all sin is the same." Clearly this is not true, according to Jesus (Matthew 10:15; 16:27; Luke 12:47-48; Revelation 22:12).

Inherently, all sin *is* sin. But not all sin carries with it the same divine consequence or punishment. Therefore, all sin is not the same. This is reflected in human morality as well. Stealing a paperclip from the office would never be considered by anyone to be as wicked as child abuse and certainly would not warrant an equal punishment. Similarly, God's righteousness will assign even greater torment in the lake of fire to those guilty of greater sins.[42]

#4 What Do the Old and New Testaments Teach About the Afterlife?

When speaking about the afterlife, we typically think of two locations—heaven and hell. But upon a closer look at the Old and New Testaments, we see that their understandings concerning where people go when they die contain meanings unique to their cultures.

In the Old Testament, the word most often used to refer to the afterlife is *sheol*. This word, used 65 times in the Old Testament, can have a variety of meanings, depending on the context. Many times, it is a synonym for "the grave," or generally, "the abode of the dead" (Genesis 37:35; 42:38; Psalm 141:7). But it can also refer to the place where the wicked are punished following death (Job 24:19; Psalm 9:17; 55:15). Sheol is pictured as being in the depths of the earth (Deuteronomy 32:22; Proverbs 15:24; Isaiah 14:15; Ezekiel 31:17). For the wicked, it is a place of darkness (Job 10:18-22; 17:13), sorrow (2 Samuel 22:6), and pain (Psalm 116:3).

But sheol can also refer to the place where the righteous go (Genesis 37:35). In this sense, it is interpreted by some as a "temporary stopping point" for Old Testament believers, though they still enjoy a heavenly presence of God there (Genesis 5:24; 2 Kings 2:11). There is no scriptural basis for the doctrine of purgatory, which is a Catholic belief. However, what exactly this version of heaven was like prior to Christ's death on the cross, we are not told. Jesus illustrated it a bit for us in Luke 16:22-23 as being in "Abraham's bosom."

In the New Testament, three words are used to convey the concept of hell: *Hades, Tartarus,* and *Gehenna. Gehenna* and *Tartarus* are typically translated as "hell." *Hades* is similar to sheol and carries over the Old Testament idea of the afterlife—realm of the dead, as well as the punishment for the unrighteous (Matthew 11:23; 16:18; Luke 10:15; 16:23; Acts 2:27,31; Revelation 1:18; 20:13-14). *Hades* is temporary and will itself be cast into the lake of fire following the great white throne judgment (Revelation 20:14).

Tartarus is used once in the New Testament (2 Peter 2:4) where it is translated as "hell." In context, it likely refers to the very bottom or worst part of hell.

Gehenna, on the other hand, has a gory symbolism attached to it. Originally the Valley of Ben-hinnom was a place located just to the southeast of the old city of Jerusalem. In Old Testament times, atrocities were routinely committed there, including the sacrifice of children to the gods Molech and Baal (Leviticus 20:2; 2 Kings 23:10; 2 Chronicles 28:3; 33:6;

Jeremiah 32:35). This prompted the prophet Jeremiah to call it "the Valley of the Slaughter" (Jeremiah 7:31-34). It was also called Topheth (7:31-32).

By New Testament times, this valley had become a place where Jerusalem's trash, dead animals, and the bodies of criminals were burned. Like the real Gehenna, Jesus said hell was a place where the fire never dies, nor does the worm that feeds on the rotting corpses (Mark 9:43-48). Christ used this word 11 times referring to the place where the unrighteous suffer.

By contrast, the portrait of heaven in the New Testament is the place where God dwells and rules (Matthew 6:9-10). It is where the "Father's house" is (John 14:1-3). All believers upon their deaths are now transported directly to heaven and into God's welcoming presence (2 Corinthians 5:6-9). More about heaven in the following questions.

#5 What Are the New Heaven and the New Earth?

Jesus made an astonishing statement in Matthew 24:35, claiming, "Heaven and earth will pass away, but My words will not pass away." Often that verse is cited to teach the eternal nature of the Word of God, and rightly so. But look again at what He is prophesying here. Heaven and earth are not eternal. In fact, they are both going to be "destroyed" by God (2 Peter 3:7-13).

So, God is going to destroy this planet, along with its atmosphere, and the present universe. And He'll do it with "a roar" (rushing sound) and with intense heat that will burn and melt the heavens and the elements down to the atomic level. Actually, the Greek word used by Peter and translated "destroyed" literally means to "unleash" or to "unbind." This strongly suggests that the elements (physical materials) are held or bound together by God's power. In fact, other Scripture reveals that God's power is holding all things together physically (Colossians 1:17). And the book of Job tells us:

> "If He were to gather His spirit and His breath to Himself,
> Humanity would perish together,
> And mankind would return to dust."
>
> (Job 34:14-15)

After this happens, the Lord creates a new kind of heaven and earth (Revelation 21:1-5), fulfilling Isaiah's prophecy (65:17). Gone forever will be the residual effects of sin and sinners.

During the millennial kingdom, the earth is restored. It experiences a renovation to offset the effects of 6,000 years of suffering and groaning, along with the tribulation judgments. But the new re-created earth bears no resemblance to its sinful predecessor. No sin will stain its inhabitants, and no demonic principalities will occupy its atmosphere. The new heavens and earth are mentioned four places in Scripture (Isaiah 65:17; 66:22; 2 Peter 3:13; Revelation 21:1). These are literal, ultra-enhanced replacements of the former heavens and earth. And what will it be like?

Revelation 21 tells us there will be no more:

- Sea (v. 1)—the geography will be radically different.
- Loneliness (v. 3)—God is with us, among us, and relationally close to us.

- Tears (v. 4)—there is nothing to cry over or to be sad about.
- Death (v. 4)—there are no sins or sinners to cause death.
- Mourning (v. 4)—sadness and sorrow are permanently erased.
- Crying (v. 4)—joy and peace are now our constant companions.
- Pain (v. 4)—all physical limitations, diseases, and sufferings have been eradicated. All these things have passed away forever.
- Thirst (v. 6)—the free water of life will perpetually satisfy us.
- Sin or sinners (vv. 8,27)—the lake of fire is consuming them in a separate location. Every wrong is made right.
- Temple (v. 22)—the Father and the Son are our temple.
- Sun, moon, or night (vv. 23-25; 22:5)—God's glory will illuminate the new earth.
- Closed gates (v. 25)—we will have eternal access to God and all that He provides.

Truly, everything will be new (21:5). What an amazing place this new creation is going to be!

#6 How Will the Eternal State Be Different from the Millennial Kingdom?

Chronologically, the thousand-year millennial kingdom exists *prior* to the eternal state. That said, there are also several other important distinctions between the two. Strictly speaking, the millennial kingdom signifies the Messiah's reign prophesied and promised to the Jewish people (Matthew 5; 13; 25). During this thousand-year kingdom, some believers will still possess their sin natures, as they have transitioned alive into the kingdom from the tribulation period. During the millennial kingdom, there will be a degree of disobedience, mostly inward, and the majority of which is from the children born during that time. This ultimately results in a large rebellion at the end (Revelation 20:7-10). However, in the eternal state, not a trace of sin or remnants of our sin nature can be found, as those tribulation believers will have been made perfect (Revelation 21:8,27).

The millennial kingdom will include a physical temple (Ezekiel 40–48), but in the eternal state, God and the Lamb are the temple (Revelation 21:22). Christ's kingdom on earth lasts for 1,000 years, but His eternal reign is...*eternal*! In both, the topography of the earth is changed. But in the new earth there is no longer any sea (Revelation 21:1).

COMPARISON
BETWEEN THE KINGDOM AND ETERNITY

MILLENNIAL KINGDOM	ETERNAL STATE
1,000 YEARS	FOREVER
TEMPLE	GOD IS OUR TEMPLE
SEA	NO MORE SEA
JERUSALEM ELEVATED	NEW JERUSALEM DESCENDS
SINFUL REBELLION	NO MORE SIN...EVER!

In the millennial kingdom, Jerusalem is elevated to a high plateau, while the surrounding mountains are turned into a massive plain (Zechariah 14:10). However, in eternity, a new Jerusalem appears, descending from heaven (Revelation 21:2). The millennial kingdom marks the last measuring of time since, going forward, time itself is swallowed into eternity. At the conclusion of the millennial kingdom, Jesus will go on reigning for all eternity (Psalm 10:16; 145:13; Lamentations 5:19; 1 Timothy 1:17; 6:13-16; Revelation 11:15).

#7 What Is the New Jerusalem?

As of 2020, the most populated city in the world is Tokyo, Japan, with over 37 million residents. With up to 20,000 people per square kilometer, over-crowding is a huge problem. But the Bible speaks of a coming city that will house countless more people than Tokyo and with zero issues with population density. This heavenly city has been the longing of believers as far back as Abraham (Hebrews 11:8-10,16; 12:22; 13:14).

Admittedly, as we take a closer look at the description of this city, it sounds a bit more science fiction than scriptural. But as bizarre as it may seem to us now, its beauty and brilliance will one day captivate our sight and senses. To begin, it's in the shape of a massive cube, measuring 1,400 miles long, 1,400 miles wide, and 1,400 miles high (Revelation 21:15-17).[43]

Mark Hitchcock helps us envision this mega city: "Think of a map of the United States. The footprint of the city would be about the same as drawing a square from Miami up to Maine then westward to Minneapolis then south to Houston and then back to Miami. And that's just the ground-level. The towering city [also] rises 1500 miles."[44]

(SHOWING SIZE, NOT FUTURE LOCATION)

John sees this cubed city descending out of the sky and resting on the earth, or perhaps hovering just above the surface. The fact that it comes down from heaven indicates that it previously existed. Some commentators speculate that during the millennial kingdom, believers who have transitioned out of the tribulation will remain on the earth while glorified Christians (us) will dwell in heaven and the new Jerusalem, having dual access to both the new Jerusalem and the earthly kingdom ("in My Father's house are many *dwelling places*," John 14:2 NASB 1995).

Prophecy scholar Ron Rhodes calculates the new Jerusalem takes up a surface area of 2,250,000 square miles, about 3,623 times the size of London, England.[45] A cube city of this size could easily accommodate some "20 million residents, each having his own private 75-acre cube."[46]

The brilliance of this city is made so by the glory of God (Revelation 21:10-12). Its walls are 216 feet thick, 1,400 miles high, and made of jasper, possibly a diamond-like material but also with a transparent golden composition and appearance (21:18). Imagine God's radiant glory shining and refracting through these magnificent walls!

There are 12 gates, each made of a single pearl (21:12,21) and guarded by angels (not Saint Peter!). Upon these gates are written the names of the 12 tribes of Israel (21:12), and they remain open for all eternity (21:25).

Twelve foundation stones are laid for the city and contain the names of the 12 apostles of the Lamb (21:14). Each is made from a different precious stone (21:19-20).

The new Jerusalem gives representation to both Israel and the church, and is a welcome home to Jew and Gentile alike, as we are united by faith in God.

There are no *streets* of gold in the new Jerusalem, but there is a single main street made of transparent pure gold (21:21). Also, the city features a river flowing out from the throne of God (22:1-2). It is called "a river of the water of life" and is "clear as crystal." It is like drinking eternal life itself.

On either side of this river is the tree of life, yielding 12 kinds of fruit every month (22:2). This reintroduces the tree Adam and Eve were prevented from accessing after being banned from the Garden of Eden (Genesis 2:9; 3:24). Its leaves are for the "healing of the nations" (22:2).[47]

The new Jerusalem is appropriately called the "holy city" as it is the place where our holy God and His holy saints dwell forever (21:2). But wait, there's more!

I (Jeff) once heard a pastor preaching on the topic of heaven. When he got to the question of what heaven would be like, he said, "God loves you. And if it's important to you, then it will be in heaven."

Um...*really*?

Is that how God decides what heaven will be like? Will there be a billion different versions of the afterlife for believers? Is heaven merely a glorified, sanctified version of Disneyworld? An eternal theme park? Upon your arrival there, do you simply go to "Insert Your Name Here" Land where you find all your wishes and dreams come true? If you're an avid golfer, will there be golf? And will you ever miss a shot? What if you're a movie buff? Is there an endless catalog of your favorite flicks for you to enjoy? Will it be like summer camp, where you can visit the ice-cream-cone stand as often as you want without fear of gaining weight? If you prefer the beach, will your "dwelling place" be on the coast?

US TRYING TO IMAGINE HEAVEN IS LIKE AN ANT TRYING TO UNDERSTAND TRIGONOMETRY.

Among the problems with imagining heaven is that we begin with us and our preferences and desires, not with Scripture. We conjure up a forever place based on our thoughts, not God's (Isaiah 55:11-12). With limited minds and understanding, we think of all the things that currently make us happy, then project that template onto our future experience in heaven. But that kind of thinking is scripturally backward...and inaccurate.

Fortunately, if we want to know what heaven is like, we only need to open the Bible. There, God paints a picture of the place Jesus has been preparing for us (John 14:1-3). We've already seen some of what it's like through looking at the new Jerusalem, but there is much more to learn, and even more to discover once we arrive. We can say this with certainty—once we are with Jesus, through death or at the rapture, we won't be worrying or wondering about what the millennium or the new Jerusalem will be like. Just being with Him will be enough.

So, heaven will not merely be what we *want* it to be. Besides, we really don't want to trust our present immature and incomplete understanding of unlimited enjoyment and satisfaction. That's because God is preparing a mind-blowing place and experience that, in a thousand lifetimes, we could not conceive of. By fantasizing about our future home with our limited understanding, we actually set ourselves up for disappointment. Instead, we develop a more genuine anticipation when we dive into Scripture and discover what it's *actually* going to be like.

So, no Chick-fil-A in heaven. Just something a billion times better!

#9 What Will We *Do* in Eternity?

If you've ever secretly feared that heaven will be one really, really long church service, then we have good news—it *won't* be. Many people claim to have taken trips to heaven, after which they return with fantastical stories about Jesus, God, the Holy Spirit, Satan, rainbow ponies, and experiences we find nowhere mentioned in God's Word. Sadly, these extrabiblical accounts mislead the bride and counterfeit the true heaven described in Scripture.

Admittedly, we all long for concrete, tangible information about what we'll be doing for the rest of eternity. That's understandable. Part of our struggle arises from an irrational fear that we might get *bored* there for that length of time. But this is impossible for two reasons: First, God cannot be boring. He is immeasurably creative and loving, and has the power to provide unimaginable happiness, adventure, enjoyment, and fulfillment. Second, boredom is a human construct, a product of a fallen humanity. It occurs when we lose interest in something and are unstimulated. Therefore, we long for something more or different. But there is nothing more or better outside of God and heaven, and our wildest imaginations cannot begin to touch what awaits us there.

So, what *can* we know? Unquestionably, some of what we will do in eternity wouldn't make sense to us if God were to tell us now. Plus, we will need glorified bodies, completed minds, and perfected souls in order to comprehend and experience all He has waiting for us there.

But among the things we *do* know we'll do in eternity are:

Serve (Revelation 22:3). As a Christian, you already know that no joy compares with what you experience when you're serving our great God. And yet this joy is presently limited because we can't see Him or physically be in His presence. But in eternity, those limitations are removed. Then we will experience the great honor and privilege of serving the King of kings. No doubt this service will involve incredible adventures!

Enjoy one another (Ecclesiastes 2:25; Matthew 8:11; 1 Thessalonians 4:17-18). Will we know each other in heaven? Yes! All the heroes of faith will be our forever friends. No conflicts or petty disagreements, but only love and depth of fellowship we cannot even imagine. Right now, our capacity for relationships is hindered by sin and human limitations. But then, the level of friendship and fellowship will be like nothing we've ever known!

Use our glorified bodies (1 Corinthians 15:20-23,42-44; 1 John 3:1-3; Revelation 1:5). Like Christ's resurrection body, our glorified bodies will possess the ability to eat and drink. But they will also withstand the intensity of heaven's atmosphere, supernaturally travel, and pass through physical objects (Luke 24:28-31; John 20:19,26; Acts 1:9-11; 1 Timothy 6:16).

Worship (Revelation 4:1-11; 5:8-14; 7:9-17). This will not be the same as the worship you've experienced when prompted by a leader on stage. Different from the worship that follows a long gaze at the night sky, or following an answered prayer, or even from studying Scripture. No. This worship will be elevated far above all previous experiences, no matter how meaningful. You will be before His throne. In His presence. And for the rest of eternity, you will be captivated by the grandeur, glory, grace, and wonder of this great God.

Be with God (John 14:3; 17:24; Revelation 21:3). More than anything, heaven is where God is. He will cover you, protect you, and love you for all eternity. "In Your presence is fullness of joy," David wrote. "In Your right hand there are pleasures forever" (Psalm 16:11). Everything will be new (Revelation 21:5).

Know God. Jesus Himself prayed in John 17:3, "This is eternal life, that they may know You, the only true God, and Jesus Christ whom You have sent." The Bible's last chapter reminds us that in the eternal new Jerusalem, "they will see His face, and His name will be on their foreheads" (Revelation 22:4).

So forget everything you've dreamed or wondered about heaven and allow God's amazing truth to fill your mind with the real thing!

#10 How Does Our Eternal Destiny Give Purpose to Our Present Lives?

It's great to think about heaven and eternity, but for right now, we're still here on earth and in our mortal bodies. We can't physically see Jesus, and we still struggle with our enemies—the world, the flesh, and the devil. We become weary, discouraged, and even defeated at times.

So, what does thinking about God's truth concerning eternity do for us right now, right in the midst of marriage, family, school, kids, jobs, friendship, and personal issues?

First, God's provision for our future is real—not imagined or invented by human minds. Jesus spoke of His Father's house as an actual "place" (John 14:2). And He promised He would take us there one day (14:3). Therefore, the reality of heaven is as solid and certain as Jesus Himself. If there is no real heaven, then Jesus is not God, because our belief about heaven is based on His Word. That declaration concerning eternity is our rock-solid guarantee (Matthew 24:35).

Second, this world is not our home. We're just passing through it on a temporary journey. Our real home, and citizenship, is in heaven (Philippians 3:20). That's where our loyalty lies. So, because this earth is just a brief blip on our eternity, we ought to spend more time setting our minds on and longing for "the things that are above, where Christ is, seated at the right hand of God. Set your minds on the things that are above, not on the things that are on earth" (Colossians 3:1-2). Learning to do this is part of our discipline for the purpose of godliness (1 Timothy 4:7). The more heavenly minded we are, the more earthly good we will do here, as we will know what really matters in eternity.

Third, our eternal destiny gives us a confident hope, knowing that "the sufferings of this present time are not worthy to be compared with the glory that is to be revealed to us" (Romans 8:18). What we face and suffer now is nothing when compared to the reward and richness of heaven. Living here and dealing with problems and pains associated with this life is like one second when measured against eternity. Life on earth is like a bump in the road; we quickly pass over it and move on. In fact, no past pain or suffering can ever impact us in eternity (Revelation 21:4-5).

Finally, thinking about heaven and eternity puts everything into its proper perspective, especially how short this life really is. That realization motivates us toward purpose and urgency. Purpose helps us focus the direction of our lives and to properly order our priorities. It helps us focus on what's right and best for us. It also protects us from mediocrity. Urgency reminds us the clock is ticking and that we have no time to waste. Whether we have five days or 50 years left, we cannot afford to squander the stewardship of time and life God has given to us. What we do now will echo and reverberate throughout all eternity!

NOTES

1. Isaiah 46:9-11.

2. Micah 5:2 and Matthew 2:1-6; Isaiah 7:14 and Matthew 1:21-23; Daniel 9:24-25 and Luke 19:37-42; Zechariah 9:9 and Matthew 21:4-5; Zechariah 11:12 and Matthew 26:14-15; Psalm 22:18 and Matthew 27:35; Psalm 22:1 and Matthew 27:46; Isaiah 53:12 and Mark 15:27-28.

3. Romans 13:11—"knowing the time (*kairos*—era, age), that it is already the hour."

   Romans 13:12—"the night is almost gone, and the day is near."

   1 Corinthians 1:7—"awaiting eagerly the revelation of our Lord Jesus Christ."

   1 Corinthians 16:22—"Maranatha" (used by the early church for "hello" or "goodbye"), from an Aramaic expression meaning "our Lord, come."

   Philippians 3:20—"heaven, from which also we eagerly wait for a Savior."

   Philippians 4:5—"the Lord is near."

   1 Thessalonians 1:10—"to wait for His Son from heaven."

   Titus 2:13—"looking for the blessed hope and the appearing of…Christ Jesus."

   Hebrews 9:28—"Christ…will appear a second time for salvation without reference to sin, to those who eagerly await Him."

   Hebrews 10:25—"encouraging one another; and all the more as you see the day drawing near."

   Hebrews 10:37—"for yet in a very little while, He who is coming will come, and will not delay."

   James 5:7-8—"Therefore be patient, brethren, until the coming of the Lord…be patient; strengthen your hearts, for the coming of the Lord is near."

   1 Peter 1:13—"fix your hope completely on the grace to be brought to you at the revelation of Jesus Christ."

   1 Peter 4:7—"The end of all things is near."

   1 John 2:18—"we know that it is the last hour."

   Jude 1:21—"waiting anxiously for the mercy of our Lord Jesus Christ."

   Revelation 3:11—"I am coming quickly; hold fast what you have."

   Revelation 22:7—"Behold, I am coming quickly."

   Revelation 22:12—"Behold, I am coming quickly."

   Revelation 22:20—"Yes, I am coming quickly."

4. J. Barton Payne, *Encyclopedia of Biblical Prophecy: The Complete Guide to Scriptural Predictions and Their Fulfillment* (New York: Harper & Row, 1973), 681-682.

5. *Secular sources*—Josephus, Tacitus, Pliny the Younger, Lucian, Phelgon, Celus, Mara Bar Serapion, Suetonius, and Thallus. *New Testament sources*—Matthew, Mark, Luke, John, Paul, author of Hebrews, James,

Peter, and Jude. *Nonbiblical Christian sources*—Clement of Rome, 2 Clement, Ignatius, Polycarp, Martyrdom of Polycarp, Didache, Barnabas, Shepherd of Hermas, Fragments of Papias, Justin Martyr, Aristides, Athenagoras, Theophilus of Antioch, Quadratus, Aristo of Pella, Melito of Sardis, Diognetus, Gospel of Peter, Apocalypse of Peter, and Epistula Apostolorum. Evan Minton, "Did Jesus Exist?," *CrossExamined .org*, September 9, 2018, https://crossexamined.org/did-jesus-exist/.

6. Luke 24:39. See also John 20:17, 20, 27-28.

7. See also Matthew 24:30.

8. This spirit of expectancy is evident in the following verses:

- Romans 13:11—"knowing the time, that it is already the hour."
- Romans 13:12—"the night is almost gone, and the day is near."
- 1 Corinthians 1:7—"awaiting eagerly the revelation of our Lord Jesus Christ."
- 1 Corinthians 16:22—"Maranatha" (used by the early church for "hello" or "goodbye," from an Aramaic expression meaning "our Lord, come").
- Philippians 3:20—"for our citizenship is in heaven, from which also we eagerly wait for a Savior."
- Philippians 4:5—"The Lord is near."
- 1 Thessalonians 1:10—"to wait for His Son from heaven."
- Titus 2:13—"looking for the blessed hope and the appearing of the glory of our great God and Savior, Christ Jesus."
- Hebrews 9:28—"so Christ also…will appear a second time for salvation without reference to sin, to those who eagerly await Him."
- Hebrews 10:25—"encouraging one another; and all the more as you see the day drawing near."
- Hebrews 10:37—"For yet in a very little while, He who is coming will come, and will not delay."
- James 5:7-8—"be patient, brethren, until the coming of the Lord…be patient; strengthen your hearts, for the coming of the Lord is near."
- 1 Peter 1:13—"fix your hope completely on the grace to be brought to you at the revelation of Jesus Christ."
- 1 Peter 4:7—"The end of all things is near."
- 1 John 2:18—"we know that it is the last hour."
- Jude 21—"waiting anxiously for the mercy of our Lord Jesus Christ."
- Revelation 3:11—"I am coming quickly; hold fast what you have."
- Revelation 22:7—"And behold, I am coming quickly."
- Revelation 22:12—"Behold, I am coming quickly."
- Revelation 22:20—"Yes, I am coming quickly."

Excerpted from Kinley, *Wake the Bride* (Eugene, OR: Harvest House Publishers, 2015), 77-79.

9. Jesus Himself claimed that every single word of God will eventually be fulfilled, even down to the punctuation marks! (Matthew 5:17-18).

10. Genesis 3:15 and Galatians 4:4; Isaiah 7:14 and Matthew 1:22-23.

11. Micah 5:2 and Matthew 2:5-6; Luke 2:4-6.

12. Zechariah 9:9 and Matthew 21:4-5.

13. Isaiah 50:6 and Matthew 26:67; 27:26.

14. Zechariah 11:12-13 and Matthew 27:9-10.

15. Psalm 22:16; Zechariah 12:10 and John 20:24-28.

16. Isaiah 53:12 and Matthew 27:38.

17. Psalm 34:20 and John 19:33-36.

18. Isaiah 53:9 and Matthew 27:57-60.

19. Psalm 16:10 and Matthew 28:1-7.

20. Peter Stoner, *Science Speaks* (Chicago: Moody Press, 1969), 106-7.

21. The point here is the principle of obedience to a specific stewardship of knowledge, not that there were two distinct dispensations (stewardships) during the church age.

22. Quote attributed to Tim LaHaye.

23. Amillennialists also typically believe Revelation was written prior to AD 70 and destruction of Jerusalem, during the reign of Nero (AD 37–68).

24. J. Barton Payne, *Encyclopedia of Biblical Prophecy: The Complete Guide to Scriptural Predictions and Their Fulfillment* (New York: Harper & Row, 1973), 477-590.

25. Thomas Ice, "A Brief History of the Rapture," *Pre-Trib Research Center*, www.pre-trib.org/articles/dr-thomas-ice/message/a-brief-history-of-the-rapture/read.

26. Thomas Ice, "A Brief History of the Rapture."

27. God told Micah that the Messiah would be born in Bethlehem, but He did not pinpoint the exact house or time (Micah 5:2). The Lord told Isaiah the Messiah would be born of a virgin, but he didn't tell him which virgin, how old she would be, or that she would already be betrothed at the time of her conception (Isaiah 7:14). Scripture gives us a detailed composite sketch of Antichrist's character and actions, but it does not tell us his identity or name.

28. Here is where *harpazo* is used in the NT, along with each meaning in context: Matthew 11:12—take by force; Matthew 12:29—carry off; Matthew 13:19—snatches away; John 6:15—take by force; John 10:12—snatch by force; John 10:28-29—snatch by force; Acts 8:39—snatch away, disappear; Acts 23:10—take away by force; 2 Corinthians 12:2—caught up to heaven; 2 Corinthians 12:4—caught up into Paradise; 1 Thessalonians 4:17—caught up…in the clouds; Jude 23—(quickly) snatching out of the fire; Revelation 12:5—(referring to Jesus) caught up to God (at the ascension).

29. The Didache was a first-century collection of teachings from the apostles, also called The Teaching of the Twelve Apostles. Chapter 16:1 reads, "Watch concerning your life; let not your lamps be quenched or your loins be loosed, but be ye ready, for ye know not the hour at which our Lord cometh."

30. Deuteronomy 30:3; Isaiah 11:11-12; 43:5-6; 66:7-8; Jeremiah 16:14-15; 30:1-22; Ezekiel 36:22-24.

31. The word *time* here is *kairos*, meaning "era, age."

32. The word *keleusma* signifies a shout of command and occurs only here in the New Testament. It was used in secular literature of an officer shouting to his troops, a charioteer to his horses, or a shipmaster to his rowers.

33. David Reagan, "The Muslim Antichrist Theory," *Lamb and Lion Ministries*, December 2010, https://christinprophecy.org/articles/the-muslim-antichrist-theory/.

34. See Matthew 24:42-47; Luke 12:35-40; Mark 13:33-37. Though these passages refer to Jesus' return at His second coming, the principles of being alert, being ready, and being prepared apply to the rapture as well.

35. Additional passages include Jeremiah 49:13-14; Daniel 11:40-45; Zechariah 12–14; Joel 3:12-17; Micah 4:11-21; Matthew 24:29-32.

36. See also Genesis 13:17; 15:7; 2 Chronicles 20:7; Acts 7:5.

37. Ralph Alexander, "Ezekiel," *The Expositor's Bible Commentary*, vol. 6, Frank E. Gaebelein, gen. ed. (Grand Rapids, MI: Zondervan, 1986), 952.

38. Mark Hitchcock, *The End* (Carol Stream, IL: Tyndale, 2012), 427.

39. In that day, Jerusalem will also be called "My holy mountain" (Psalm 2:6; Isaiah 11:9), "The Throne of the LORD" (Jeremiah 3:17), "Zion" and "Mount Zion" (Joel 3:16-17; Micah 4:7), "chief of the mountains" (Micah 4:1), and "the City of Truth" (Zechariah 8:2-3).

40. See Question 5 regarding worship in the millennial kingdom and an explanation of animal sacrifices during that time.

41. *Joy*—Isaiah 9:3; 12:3-6; 14:7-8; 25:8-9; 30:29; 42:1; Jeremiah 30:18-19; Zephaniah 3:14-17; Zechariah 8:19; 10:6-7; *peace*—Isaiah 2:4-9; 9:4-7; 11:6-9; Zechariah 9:10; *holiness*—Isaiah 4:3-4; 29:19; 35:8; 52:1; *justice* and *righteousness*—Isaiah 9:7; 11:1-5; 32:16; 42:1-4; 60:21; 65:21-33; Jeremiah 31:23; Ezekiel 37:23-24; Zephaniah 3:1,13; *health*—Isaiah 29:18; 33:24; 35:5-6; 61:1-2; 65:20; Ezekiel 34:16.

42. In the same manner, there will also be varying degrees of reward in heaven. All those who trust in Christ will be saved, but some will "suffer loss" regarding their reward, and yet "he himself will be saved" (1 Corinthians 3:10-15). Others will receive much praise and reward from Jesus Christ (1 Corinthians 4:5; 9:24-27; 2 Corinthians 5:10; 1 Thessalonians 2:19; 2 Timothy 4:7-8; James 1:12; 1 Peter 5:4; Revelation 2:10).

43. The holy of holies in Solomon's temple was also cube shaped, perhaps here signifying that this new Jerusalem serves as God's eternal dwelling place (1 Kings 6:20).

44. Hitchcock, *The End*, 454.

45. Ron Rhodes, *The End Times in Chronological Order* (Eugene, OR: Harvest House, 2012), 223.

46. Ibid.

47. The word *healing* is the Greek word *therapeia*, from which we get our English word *therapeutic*. Since there will be no disease or pain or death or soreness in the new Jerusalem, these leaves must somehow enhance our heavenly enjoyment, possibly through eating them. John MacArthur writes that they may somehow serve as "supernatural vitamins." John MacArthur, *The MacArthur New Testament Commentary: Revelation 12–22* (Chicago: Moody Press, 2000), 287.

From the team behind the Prophecy Pros Podcast comes *A Quick Reference Guide to the End Times*—a concise look at the most pressing questions about the rapture, the Antichrist, the millennial kingdom, and beyond. Jeff and Todd share their wealth of Scripture-based knowledge about the end times, steering away from speculation to make sure you get only the information that truly matters.

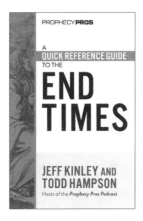

Featuring helpful charts, graphics, and illustrations, this accessible manual will help you understand answers to important prophecy questions such as...

- in what basic order will the end times unfold?
- how do we know Jesus is literally returning to earth?
- how should Christians live if Jesus might return any day now?

Whether you're totally new to Bible prophecy or you've been studying it for years, *A Quick Reference Guide to the End Times* is the user-friendly handbook you need to keep track of the most essential facts about the future.